Best Loop Hikes Wisconsin

Best Loop Hikes
Wisconsin

A Guide to the State's Greatest Loop Hikes

Steve Johnson

GUILFORD, CONNECTICUT

FALCONGUIDES®

An imprint of Globe Pequot, the trade division of The Rowman & Littlefield Publishing Group, Inc.
4501 Forbes Blvd., Ste. 200
Lanham, MD 20706
www.rowman.com

Falcon and FalconGuides are registered trademarks and Make Adventure Your Story is a trademark of The Rowman & Littlefield Publishing Group, Inc.

Distributed by NATIONAL BOOK NETWORK

Copyright © 2022 The Rowman & Littlefield Publishing Group, Inc.

Photos by Steve Johnson unless otherwise noted
Maps by Melissa Baker © The Rowman & Littlefield Publishing Group, Inc.

British Library Cataloguing in Publication Information available

Library of Congress Cataloging-in-Publication Data available

ISBN 978-1-4930-5797-9 (paperback)
ISBN 978-1-4930-5798-6 (electronic)

♾™ The paper used in this publication meets the minimum requirements of American National Standard for Information Sciences—Permanence of Paper for Printed Library Materials, ANSI/NISO Z39.48-1992.

The author and The Rowman & Littlefield Publishing Group, Inc. assume no liability for accidents happening to, or injuries sustained by, readers who engage in the activities described in this book.

Contents

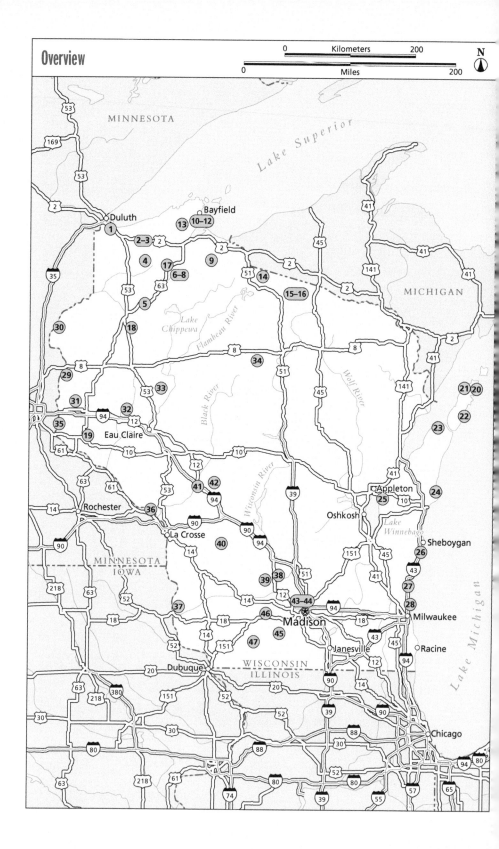

Overview

Introduction

Cheese, cows, and idyllic farmsteads tucked among sinuous hillsides of emerald green or fiery autumn yellow. Fluffy snow, ice-cold brew, and skiing. Deep coulees along the western border are living postcards. Lake Superior, cabins, and the resplendent Northwoods. These are just a few of our favorite things here in Wisconsin.

We boast 1,000 miles of Great Lakes shoreline to the north and east, and inland we have more than 15,000 lakes in a variety of shapes and sizes. Wisconsin also has nearly 13,000 rivers and streams, some small and quiet, others big and noisy. Did you know our state's name is derived from a river? In Native Miami language, "Meskousing" is a river name that passed through French explorers and a transcription error to arrive at "Wisconsin." Who'd a thunk it?

My favorite way to explore Wisconsin's outdoorsy accoutrements is on foot, exploring hiking trails through the wilds, even better on a loopy path that is shiny and new with every step. A loop hike is a special treat. Every trail has its own unique characteristics, a personality, if you will, and there is something inherently mysterious about hiking a loop trail for the first time. It's like meeting a new friend, discovering their ups and downs and learning their hidden secrets. Best of all, it's about being together and having a good ol' time. The anticipation of the unknown, the exploration of a new place, finding hidden treasures around each bend and over every knoll. On a loop trail, newfound territory never ends, and it's like hiking the path for the first time, all the time.

Join me on a tour of Wisconsin, from bucolic, rolling countryside in the state's midsection to the Driftless Area's magic kingdom of bluffs and deep valleys. Explore vibrant cities, charming small towns, Door County's legendary vibe, and breathe deeply of the incomparable northern forests. The hikes in these chapters take you up close with some of the state's most dramatic scenery.

This book is arranged by region generally from north to south and highlights the state's showiest environs. A "best of" book is ultimately subjective, of course, implying that its contents include the finest examples of its title subject. I get to do it because my name's on the cover and while you might wonder why your favorite hike isn't included or what makes my choices so great, I'm sharing with you places that genuinely inspired me and that I believe best represent our amazing state. There are dozens more that will make a great sequel! Caveat: To appeal to the widest possible audience, most hikes herein are less than 10 miles in length and manageable in a couple of hours or an afternoon. Many locations, however, include longer options or are close to trails of extended distance (think North Country and Ice Age Trails).

Each entry is introduced by an information block outlining the name and location of the trail, hike distance and difficulty, applicable maps, GPS coordinates and directions for trailheads, contact information, and other beta. As far as gear and supplies, the best thing about these hikes is there are no complicated gear concerns. Just

Boardwalk trail at Lion's Den Gorge

throw on decent footwear and proper clothing and away you go. Plan ahead though to make each visit a good one. Expect weather common to the area and pack accordingly. Bring extra water in the humid heat of summer and be ready for cold winds and impromptu rainstorms, especially near the big lakes. On longer hikes your feet will be happier inside sturdy shoes or hiking boots and be sure to take along snacks or a veritable grocery cart of grub for picnics at trailside overlooks or wooded campsites. Don't forget a camera or other photo device to take home the sights and sounds of wherever you may roam.

And stay safe, please. Sometimes it's just plain irresistible to take one more step for a closer look, but that urge, especially near rivers and gorges, might send you on a long fall to a really hard or really wet landing. Oh, and I must mention mosquitoes. If you're from here, you know the tale; if you're visiting, heed the following: In summer months anywhere in or near a forest, lake, or even puddle, be sure to hike at least a step or two faster than the airspeed velocity of skeeters, lest the savage creatures gather upon you, mercilessly extract your lifeblood, and leave you like a withered, airless balloon. (That's only partly embellished; no kidding, the bugs can be bad.) Wear strategic gear and never, ever forget insect repellent.

Trail Etiquette

What better way to wander the land than with a good hike? Tuck your feet into a faithful pair of boots, find a favorite trail, and just go. Sure, hiking gets us out there in a wonderful, uninhibited escape, but we still need to use our noggins on occasion to share the outdoor experience. A little common sense and good old-fashioned courtesy

Elevated Lake Michigan views

go a long way to ensure a good time for everyone. Chances are good you will cross paths with other user groups, such as mountain bikers, horseback riders, trail runners, or folks hiking with dogs. All of us need to recreate responsibly with a keen respect for the environment to preserve the trails we enjoy so much, especially in the backcountry. That said, here are a few reminders to take along on your next trek.

When meeting other hikers on the trail, give those traveling uphill the right-of-way. The ascending hiker is often focused on the trail immediately ahead to scan for obstacles or maintain a steady pace and might not even see a downhill traveler until they nearly bonk heads. It is also easier for descending hikers to rein in their strides and give the uphill group room to keep on truckin'.

Horseback riders have the right of way all the time, regardless of which direction they are heading. Hikers should exit the trail, on the downhill side if possible, to avoid intimidating the horses, and talk to the riders as they pass. Don't stand behind trees or other concealing foliage, either; a spooked horse can instantly switch gears from a leisurely clip-clop to full-out, homestretch sprint.

Being more mobile, hikers can easily yield to trail runners and mountain bikers, as well, both of whom rapidly overtake our slower pace. While traditional practice sees bikes yield to boots, it is often wiser to step aside and let cyclists pass, instead of expecting bikers to ride around you, causing them to go off trail or dismount and get their steeds out of the way.

Along with good manners, we should also remember to tread lightly in our travels and practice minimum impact. Be familiar with and live the Leave No Trace principles of outdoor travel.

Camping

When ambling along a trail in the wilderness, with crystal skies and cool mountain air, not much else could make it better, except maybe one thing: staying longer. Most of the hikes in this book are day trips, from just a quick couple of miles to an afternoon's worth, but many of them also have opportunities for camping. Throwing down a tent in perfect solitude gives us a seamless outdoor experience and can add a whole new page of memories. Seeing as how we are sensible outdoor enthusiasts, we carry our "tread lightly" habits from the trail to the campsite, too. Low-impact camping has all kinds of benefits—for us, for other users, for local flora and fauna, and especially for the land itself. Here are a few handy tips:

- Use an established tent site whenever available. These sites position campers in areas least likely to trample fragile vegetation or cause erosion. If no site is available, choose an area with rocky or sandy soil.

- When it comes to personal business, backcountry bathroom efforts require slight changes in your usual routine. If there is an outhouse in the vicinity, use it. An outdoor loo is there to keep nature tidy and clean. If no toilet is available, head far from the campsite and any creeks, trails, or lakes; dig a hole 6 to 8 inches deep; and do your thing. When finished, bury the waste with the previously removed dirt and cover with leaves and sticks.

- Resist the urge to build a campfire. In many areas of Wisconsin and at different times of the year, campfires are not allowed for several reasons, the obvious being to prevent starting a devastating forest fire. Frequent scavenger hunts for firewood eventually denude the area of downfall, which serves as food and habitat for lots of little critters. Bring a camp stove and save the fires for parks with designated pits.

- Hold fast to the "pack it in, pack it out" edict. Everything you bring should stay with you for the entire trip and all the way back to the trailhead (except the stuff buried in the hole).

Hiking is an activity that goes beyond the traditional goal of physical exercise. It allows us close contact with our favorite places, a chance to reach out, and for the land to reach in with a comforting hand. The beauty of Wisconsin beckons for a time of reflection or to challenge our spirit. A trek to a quiet Northwoods lake, for example, is the perfect place. Indeed, a pair of boots and a pack can do wonders for easing life's ills or satisfying a case of wanderlust. It's always recess in Wisconsin's playground. Come wander in circles!

A final note before you hit the trails: I included a "Why Go?" callout for each hike in the book. I am forever fascinated by what's behind the scenes of what's out there, a place's history or rare or endangered plants and animals within. Most of all, I feel a keen connection to the significance of Wisconsin's special places and wanted to share that with you. We have an extraordinary privilege to connect with and enjoy nature at its finest; I hope you enjoy learning a little more of our state's very best.

How to Use This Guide

This a fun book with zest matching its subject matter. You will find this guide contains just about everything you need to choose, plan for, and enjoy a Wisconsin loop hike. Packed with specific area information, *Best Loop Hikes Wisconsin* features nearly sixty mapped and cued hikes leading to some of our state's most enticing outdoor trappings, grouped together geographically. Here is an outline of the book's major components:

Each hike starts with a short **summary** of the hike's highlights. These quick overviews give you a taste of the hiking adventures and featured locations. You'll learn about trail terrain and what unforgettable sights each route has to offer. Following the overview are **hike specs**—quick, nitty-gritty details of not only the lake or river but also the hike to it.

Distance: The total distance of the recommended route.

Hiking time: The average time it will take to cover the route. It is based on the total distance, elevation gain, and condition and difficulty of the trail. Your fitness level will also affect your time.

Photogenic factor: This is a 1 to 5 rating, with 5 being slack-jaw gorgeous.

Difficulty: Each hike has been assigned a level of difficulty—easy, moderate, or challenging. The rating system was developed from several sources and personal experience. These levels are meant to be guidelines only and may prove easier or harder for different people depending on ability and physical fitness. For purposes of this book, an easy hike will generally cover 2 miles or less total trip distance, with minimal elevation gain and a paved or smooth-surfaced dirt trail. A moderate hike will cover 3 to 8 miles total trip distance in one day, with moderate elevation gain and potentially rough terrain. A challenging hike may cover up to 10 miles total trip distance in one day, have significant elevation gains, and/or have rough and/or rocky terrain.

Trail surface: General information about what to expect underfoot.

Other trail users: This includes information on frequent users of the trail, such as horseback riders, mountain bikers, inline skaters, etc.

Canine compatibility: Know the trail regulations before you take your dog hiking with you. Dogs are typically allowed when leashed for the hikes in this book.

Land status: City park, state park, national park, or forest, etc.

Fees and permits: Denotes park entrance fees and permits, if any.

Maps: This is a list of other maps to supplement the maps in this book. USGS maps are the best source for accurate topographical information, but local park maps may show trails that are more recent. Use both.

Trail contacts: This is the location, phone number, and website for the local land manager(s) in charge of all the trails within the selected hike. Get trail access information before you head out or contact the land manager after your visit if you see problems with trail erosion, damage, or misuse.

Horizon-wide views

The **Finding the trailhead** section provides dependable driving directions to trailheads. This also includes GPS trailhead coordinates for accurate navigation.

The hike is the meat of the chapter. Detailed and honest, it is a carefully researched impression of the area and the hike, and interesting things you may see along the way, both natural and human.

Miles and Directions mileage cues identify all turns and trail-name changes, as well as points of interest.

Sidebars are found throughout the book and are quick and often fascinating facts about the locale.

A detailed and expertly crafted **map** is included with each hike and is derived from GPS tracks and related field data collected while on the hikes.

Enjoy your outdoor exploration of Wisconsin's beauty, and remember to pack out what you pack in.

How to Use the Maps

The **overview map** shows the location of each hike in the area by hike number. The **route maps** are the primary guides to each hike. They show the hike featured, all the access roads and trails, points of interest, water, landmarks, and geographical features. They also distinguish trails from roads, and paved roads from unpaved roads. The selected routes are highlighted, and directional arrows point the way.

Trail Finder

To help readers get started on the hikes best suited to their interests and abilities, this trail finder categorizes each of the hikes into a helpful list organized by hike number and name. Hikes may appear in more than one category.

Hike #/name	Best hikes for water lovers (views and/or access)	Best hikes for great views	Secluded locales	Kid-friendly hikes	Best hikes for backpackers
1 Amnicon Falls State Park	■			■	
2 Stony Hill Nature Trail		■	■	■	
3 Old Bayfield Road Trail		■	■		
4 Tomahawk Lake Trails	■		■	■	
5 Hayward Recreational Forest			■	■	
6 Forest Lodge Nature Trail			■		■
7 Hildebrand Lake Trail	■		■		■
8 Porcupine Lake Wilderness			■	■	■
9 Copper Falls State Park	■	■		■	■
10 Big Ravine Trail	■	■		■	

Hike #/name	Best hikes for water lovers (views and/or access)	Best hikes for great views	Secluded locales	Kid-friendly hikes	Best hikes for backpackers
11 Madeline Island—Big Bay State Park			■	■	■
12 Mount Ashwabay—Trogdor Trail	■	■	■		
13 Mount Valhalla Trails			■	■	
14 North Lakeland Discovery Center	■			■	
15 Escanaba Lake Trail	■		■	■	
16 Plum Lake Hemlock Forest SNA	■		■		■
17 Drummond Loop		■	■		
18 Hunt Hill Audubon Sanctuary	■	■	■	■	
19 Nugget Lake Trails	■	■	■	■	
20 Newport State Park	■	■	■	■	
21 Nicolet Loop—Peninsula State Park	■	■		■	
22 Whitefish Dunes State Park	■	■		■	
23 Potawatomi State Park	■	■		■	

Hike #/name	Best hikes for water lovers (views and/or access)	Best hikes for great views	Secluded locales	Kid-friendly hikes	Best hikes for backpackers
24 Point Beach State Forest	■	■		■	
25 High Cliff State Park		■	■	■	
26 Kohler-Andrae State Park	■	■		■	
27 Lion's Den Gorge	■	■	■	■	
28 Milwaukee Lakefront Trail	■	■		■	
29 Falls Bluff Loop–Osceola	■	■		■	
30 Sandrock Cliffs	■	■		■	
31 Willow River State Park	■	■	■	■	
32 Hoffman Hills Recreation Area		■	■		
33 Chippewa Moraine SRA–Circle Trail	■		■	■	■
34 Timms Hill		■		■	
35 Kinnickinnic State Park	■	■		■	
36 Perrot State Park	■	■	■		

Hike #/name	Best hikes for water lovers (views and/or access)	Best hikes for great views	Secluded locales	Kid-friendly hikes	Best hikes for backpackers
37 Wyalsusing State Park	■	■	■		
38 Devil's Lake State Park	■	■			
39 Natural Bridge State Park	■	■			
40 Wildcat Mountain State Park			■	■	
41 Castle Mound Nature Trail		■		■	
42 Wildcat Mound–Smrekar Trails	■			■	
43 Lakeshore Nature Preserve–UW Madison	■			■	
44 University of Wisconsin Arboretum	■	■	■		
45 New Glarus Woods State Park			■		
46 Blue Mound State Park		■			
47 Yellowstone Lake State Park	■	■			

Map Legend

Municipal

≡70≡ Interstate Highway

≡160≡ US Highway

≡105≡ State Road

≡CR96≡ County/Forest Road

= = = = Unpaved Road

⊢—•—⊣ Railroad

•—•—•— Powerline

------- State Boundary

Trails

------- Featured Trail

———— Paved Trail

------ Trail

Water Features

Lake/Reservoir

River/Creek

Intermittent Stream

Rapids

Waterfall

Symbols

⌣ Bridge

▲ Campground

•—• Gate

⌣ Pass

▲ Peak

🅰 Picnic Area

■ Point of Interest/Structure

🅿 Ranger Station

🚻 Restrooms

○ Town

① Trailhead

🖼 Viewpoint/Overlook

❓ Visitor/Information Center

💧 Water

Land Management

National Park/Forest/
Historic Site

National Monument/
Wilderness Area/Grassland

Open Space/Recreation Area/
Conservation Area/Study Area

State/Local Park

Far North and Lake Superior

I only went for a walk and finally concluded to stay out till sundown, for going out, I found, was really going in.

John Muir

I f you're from here, you know the feeling, that swell of pride, respect, awe, allure. Whether for a single visit or a lifetime, seeing the big lake, plying its waters, feeling its pulse, is an indelible memory. Call it a siren song, sentiment, challenge, peace—for anyone hailing from the Northland, Lake Superior is part of

Frels Lake

our lives. The lake captivated me as a toddler and its spell remains strong in my heart. I've brought many friends and first-timers to its shores and all left here fascinated, inspired, and humbled by this legendary inland sea. Superior is stunningly beautiful. It is deep and icy cold, moody and seductive. To me, it is a maelstrom, peaceful inspiration, confidante. It is the *Edmund Fitzgerald* and campfires and hiking.

Lake Superior grabs ahold of its admirers in a hypnotic embrace; it is a young child discovering agates and polished round rocks at Wisconsin Point one day, and a seasoned freighter crew grappling with 20-foot swells the next. Indeed, as we are traditionally, instinctively, excitedly inclined to do around here, we love to get out into the wild to feel and touch and smell, and Gitchi Gummi delivers all of that and so much more.

In winter the big lake heaves and growls as its deathly cold waters toss 3-foot-thick ice blocks in chaotic piles along the shore and shipping lanes. Come October and November, furious storms turn Superior into a howling rage, tossing thousand-foot ships like bathtub toys and slamming roiling, frothy waves into anything in their way before reluctantly surrendering to battered but stalwart shoreline. Indeed, it is an incredible, life-list experience to be near the lake when it turns wild and surly, and I highly recommend a front-row seat.

The magic doesn't end with the water, however. Lake Superior's southern shore is a venerable conduit to adventure, boasting more than 300 miles of drop-dead gorgeous scenic sights, quaint villages, and verdant forests—millions of acres of decadent woods filled with towering pines, bright white birch, tick-ticking aspen leaves, noble oaks, and remnant old growth hemlock. Soft drapes of moss embrace ancient fallen logs, slender creeks dance over rocks and through rugged ravines, and through it all wander trails of mystery and adventure, inspiration and reflection. On a long and sinuous journey from the Twin Ports to Bayfield and the Apostle Islands, you can travel through lands of quiet bays; high, rugged cliffs; and scenic rivers. In springtime, boisterous rivers blast over crests of high cliffs into splendiferous vistas. Autumn is tranquil creeks whispering beneath aged bridges and past secret hideaways.

It is a place to engage with what matters most. Whatever that may be for you, you'll find it up here in the Northland.

1 Amnicon Falls State Park

This popular state park boasts a splendid mix of waterfalls, aromatic pine-cedar forest, a historic bridge, and old sandstone quarry. Be sure to plan lunch at one of the riverside picnic sites.

Distance: 1.9 miles, with options for additional miles
Difficulty: Easy
Photogenic factor: 4
Hiking time: 45 minutes
Trail surface: Packed dirt
Other trail users: None
Canine compatibility: Leashed pets allowed

Land status: State park
Fees and permits: Vehicle pass required
Maps: State park map; USGS South Range
Trail contacts: Amnicon Falls State Park, 4279 South CR U, South Range, WI 54874; (715) 398-3000; https://dnr.wisconsin.gov/topic/parks/amnicon

Finding the trailhead: From the junction of US 2/53, follow US 2 east 0.8 mile to CR U and turn left. Head north 0.3 mile to the park entrance. **Trailhead GPS:** N46 60.899' / W92 89.216'

The Hike

If you were around this area 9,000 years ago, you could have hiked with mastodons. The great beasts followed receding glaciers and ran from the spears of early nomadic hunters. Later, American Indians made homes along the Great Lakes, followed by waves of European settlers establishing brand-new lives and occupations. Many of these hardy souls trapped beaver, mink, and otter along the Amnicon River, trading their haul with resident American Indians. Right around 1850, the promise of copper mining riches lured even more people to northern Wisconsin lands. Their efforts largely failed, but successful lumberjacks reveled in harvesting vast swaths of pine, leveraging the Amnicon's powerful spring flow to float logs to Lake Superior and onward to sawmills across the north.

Today's state park and surrounding area also boast a rich geologic history, largely focused on the Douglas Fault and brownstone. The former is a 500-million-year-old upheaval of basalt bedrock stretching from Ashland to just northeast of Minneapolis. Furious volcanic eruptions created the fault and accompanying rock formations visible at the park's Upper and Lower Falls. Sandstone exposed from the melee inspired another industry steeped in Wisconsin's late 1800s history. A constellation of quarries in this part of the state extracted more than one million cubic feet of brownstone, a sandstone relative wildly popular as building blocks for grand architecture in nearby Superior and Duluth, as well as the Twin Cities, Chicago, Omaha, and other Midwestern locales. A remnant quarry site is located northwest of Amnicon's Thimbleberry Nature Trail, this book's first hike.

Lower Falls below Horton Bridge

From the trailhead, you'll notice straight away that this is a popular place. Decades of footsteps have tamped paths to a smooth sheen and denuded many areas of foliage. Even so, soaring pines and aromatic cedar flanking the river remain splendidly elegant, and it's easy to see what attracted generations of visitors to this special place. The waterfalls, of course, are the feature attraction, fueled by the root-beer-colored Amnicon River, a state-designated Outstanding Resource Water flowing 45 miles from its headwaters at Amnicon Lake. Easygoing trails lead along the river and across a short footbridge to close-up views of Upper Falls, dropping about ten feet over bulbous basalt. After a brief respite in a shallow pool, the river flows beneath Horton Bridge, a handsome, 55-foot span above Lower Falls. One of only five others known of its kind, the bridge was inspired by Wisconsin inventor Charles Horton, who incorporated arched support beams and hooks to create an efficient and visibly stunning design. The bridge originally served as a county highway river crossing and was moved to its present location in 1930, donning a roof 9 years later.

Trails on either side of the bridge allow for all manner of casual exploring among spectacular scenery of the narrow river gorge. After an exhilarating "warm-up" at the main falls, follow the well-trod path above the river to Snake Pit Falls, a slender cascade housed in an intimate grotto of rugged grey rock and emerald-green pine. From here, retrace your tracks to the trailhead and walk the road to the start of the Thimbleberry Nature Trail, adjacent to the park office.

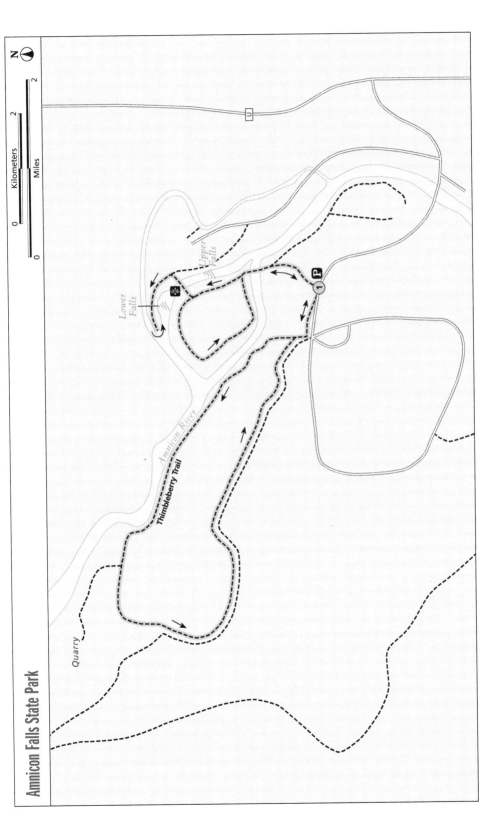

Ammicon Falls State Park

Upper Falls

Lower Falls

Ammicon River

Thimbleberry Trail

Quarry

N

Kilometers   2

Miles

0   2

Upper Falls (left); fall colors dress up an old pine snag (right)

The trail descends gently toward the river, with here-and-there views through the trees. Interpretive signs appear at regular intervals, announcing a variety of fascinating facts about the forest and area history. For example, did you know the northern white cedar is high in vitamin C? The tree's natural elixir was frequently used by the Ojibwe people, who also offered it to French explorers stricken with scurvy. Visitors today can also turn to the basswood, should their GORP supplies run dry. The sap and leaves make a reliable food source and its flowers make a nutritious tea. Run out of rope? A basswood's bark can be braided into twine and rope.

Look for red columbine and various fern species on the forest floor, along with colorful wildflowers in early summer, such as purple vetch, white pea, and pink pyrola. The vetch was a go-to food source and salve for American Indians, and pyrola contain ingredients that mitigate pain and swelling from injury or sickness. Beyond its outer beauty, the forest is full of healing properties and so many mysteries yet unknown.

About one mile in, a spur trail leads northwest to the old sandstone quarry site, while the main path curves into a small, open meadow, lingering only briefly before ascending a moderate elevation rise back into the woods. Walk quietly and stop often; this is a great place to spot resident wildlife like porcupine, ruffed grouse, coyote, fox, deer, songbirds, and lots more. Look for tracks on the ground, too, and likely critter homesites in old logs, snags, and hillsides. The trail loops southeasterly over barely there undulations back to the trailhead.

Why Go?

The Amnicon Falls-Pattison State Park research region is made of a mosaic of coastal plain, forest upland, wetlands, streams, and rivers. Largely remote, these areas coagulate to provide connectivity with adjacent lands, and that means critical habitat and migration corridors for a rich diversity of wildlife species. The gray wolf and pine marten, for example, have utilized wilderness and roadless areas in moving from Minnesota to Wisconsin. State management plans continue studies and plan implementation to direct similar success in future plant and animal populations.

Miles and Directions

0.0 Set off from the trailhead to immediate views of the river. Follow the trail across a short footbridge adjacent to Upper Falls and cross Horton Bridge. Enjoy river and gorge views on that side and cross the bridge again, this time following the trail to the right, into the woods.

0.4 Pass Snake Pit Falls and return to and pass the trailhead to the park road. Follow the road to Thimbleberry Nature Trail.

0.7 Start Thimbleberry Nature Trail.

1.0 Pass spur trail to quarry site.

1.8 Complete Thimbleberry Loop.

1.9 Arrive back at the trailhead.

Autumn on the Amnicon

2 Stony Hill Nature Trail

Score a choice campsite and top it off with this short hike through quintessential North Country forest to the summit of Stony Hill and linger-worthy (foliage permitting) view of the Brule River Valley.

Distance: 1.8 miles
Difficulty: Easy with some moderate climbing
Photogenic factor: 4
Hiking time: 40-60 minutes
Trail surface: Packed dirt and spongy pine needle turf
Other trail users: None
Canine compatibility: Leashed pets allowed

Land status: State forest
Fees and permits: None
Maps: State forest map; USGS Brule
Trail contacts: Brule River State Forest, 6250 South Ranger Rd., Brule, WI 54820; (715) 372-5678; dnr.wi.gov/topic/StateForests/BruleRiver

Finding the trailhead: From Brule, follow WI 27 south 0.83 mile to Hatchery Road. Turn right and head south and west 1.1 miles to Ranger Road. Turn left and the trailhead is at the end of the road, 0.5 mile on the left. **Trailhead GPS:** N46 53.787' / W91 59.284'

The Hike

The Bois Brule River (translated from Ojibwe meaning "burnt wood") is a revered and storied waterway, with hundreds of years of tales to tell. The ancestors of the birch trees along the riverbanks provided inspiration—and raw materials—for the earliest canoes of the Chippewa. The intrepid voyageurs followed during the heady days of the fur trade. Close behind were headstrong miners and tireless lumbermen, plying the waters and surrounding forests in their trades. Canoeists on the Brule today enjoy the same postcard scenery around every bend, including a few colossal white pines soaring skyward, providing ideal perch and nesting sites for bald eagles.

I've mentioned the Brule with affection and reverence on many occasions in my books, and this chapter celebrates the river from on high. This short, exhilarating hike leads to the top of Stony Hill with an overlook perched above the river valley for a predictably stunning view of Little Joe and Doodlebug Rapids far below. (Keep in mind dense summer foliage renders the scene slightly less beauteous.) Yes, a couple of hundred feet of elevation gain is hardly worth mentioning for those accustomed to topography in, say, the Rockies or Sierras, and this trail's uphill trajectory is a gradual undertaking. Nevertheless, you should be prepared to hoof it a bit.

Breathing deep of the forest's smells and spirit is sweet elixir in its own right, and this trail complements the experience with interpretive signs packed with engaging information and stories about this area's rich history. In fact, hiking the loop clockwise (as related here) takes you on a past-to-present tour while counter-clockwise is a back-in-time trek. From the trailhead, the cozy trail curves gently through a stand of skyscraping red and white pines on delightfully spongy tread made of layers of pine needles and organic duff. In short order, the path ramps up and continues its winding course through a mix of pine, birch, aspen, and scattered oak.

Take a moment to reflect on the proud and deep past of the Sioux and Chippewa people living here long before the appearance of European explorers and settlers. The river valley provided abundant hunting grounds and locations to establish camps, two ingredients that also attracted fur traders that leveraged the Brule as a critical route inland. One legendary explorer, Daniel Greysolon du Lhut was tasked with traveling here to inspire peace between the Sioux and Chippewa and ensure continued success of the fur trade. As time passed, the Brule valley was "controlled" by the French, English, and eventually the US. The advance of railroads ushered in hordes of new settlers in the 1800s, with the Northern Pacific linking St. Paul to Duluth in 1870 and then eastward to Brule and Ashland. Another track crossed the Brule River near Winneboujou, escorting passenger trains between Marquette, Michigan, and Duluth.

Along the trail are markers emblazoned with a bare left foot for a fun take on leading the way, and they soon take you to the summit of Stony Hill. A pair of benches await for extended lingering and ogling time of the valley—if the insects allow it. It's no secret that mosquitoes fancy these woods, too, and celebrate the appearance of warm-blooded hikers. When hiking this trail in the summer months, be ready with bug spray and remember your window for rest stops or views is extremely short, as the voracious creatures will descend upon you.

The trail shares company with mystical pines

Hikers dwarfed by sky-high white pines (left); on the way to Stony Hill (right)

The last stretch of trail from Stony Hill is naturally downhill, for an easy cruise back to the trailhead. Along the way you'll pass an interpretive sign telling about Wisconsin's logging era; about how the state was a world leader in lumber production with more than 3.5 billion board feet produced every year. Rivers and rail lines transported raw timber until it was all gone and the barren land sold to immigrants for farming (which ultimately failed). The "all gone" part can be difficult to grasp, as splendid as the forests look today. It was nothing short of annihilation of magnificent land, left for dead after humans took what they wanted to make a buck. It's a shame that nothing has changed and that this mindset still pervades, but we cling to hope with the exemplary work being done by those of far sight and determined mind. For example, back in 1903, Wisconsin's first state forester, E.M. Griffith, initiated sustainable forestry here. And it works—sustainable forest management employs selective cutting to bolster populations of robust species and introduce others through plantings. The Brule River corridor is steadily returning to its natural state, while mixing responsible harvesting with strategic ecosystem protection.

Why Go?

The Brule River State Forest hosts three distinct ecosystems—Lake Superior Clay Plain, Mille Lacs Uplands, and Bayfield Sand Plain, making for a highly diverse landscape that includes more than forty endangered and threatened animal species. The area also retains a unique potential for restoration of boreal forest spruce-fir cover, along with pine, birch, cedar, maple, aspen, and tamarack.

Stony Hill Nature Trail

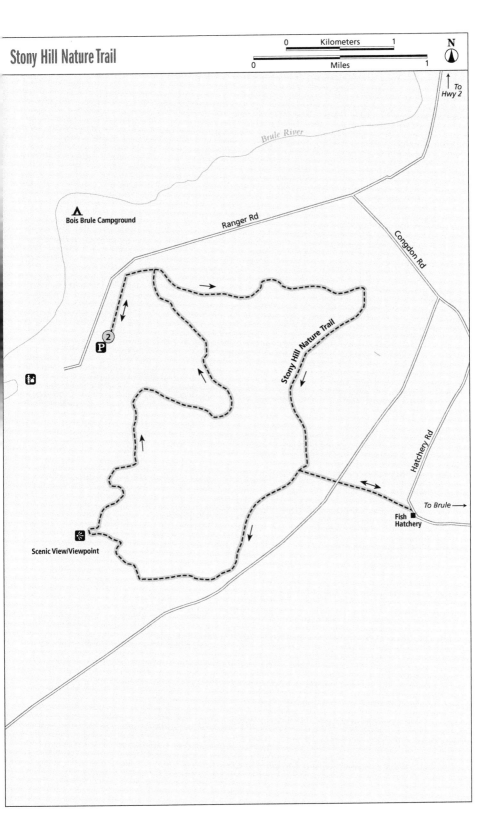

0 Kilometers 1

0 Miles 1

N

To Hwy 2

Brule River

Bois Brule Campground

Ranger Rd

Congdon Rd

2

P

Stony Hill Nature Trail

Hatchery Rd

To Brule →

Fish Hatchery

Scenic View/Viewpoint

Just follow your toes

Miles and Directions

0.0 From the trailhead, set off into the woods on an easterly course, with one short uphill ramp.

0.4 The trail turns southbound and begins a long, gradual climb.

1.1 Arrive at the top of Stony Hill.

1.8 Arrive back at the trailhead.

THE RIVER OF PRESIDENTS

In addition to its extraordinary beauty, the Brule River is a world-class fishing stream. Lively trout and the area's sublime solitude attracted five US presidents to Cedar Island Lodge, a rustic retreat on an especially scenic bend in the river. Presidents Grant, Cleveland, Coolidge, Hoover, and Eisenhower spent time here relaxing on retreats from their demanding jobs. In fact, Coolidge enjoyed the "summer White House" so much he stayed nearly the entire summer of 1928, relaxing and occasionally tending to political matters. A high school in Superior, 30 miles away, was transformed into a presidential business hub and the school's library became Coolidge's temporary Oval Office.

3 Old Bayfield Road Trail

Hike along part of the original road that linked Bayfield and Superior in the late 1800s that offers long-distance views of sprawling forest and the fringe of Lake Superior.

Distance: 2.6 miles
Difficulty: Moderate with some gradual climbing
Photogenic factor: 4
Hiking time: 50-60 minutes
Trail surface: Hard packed dirt with some grassy sections and boardwalk
Other trail users: None

Canine compatibility: Leashed pets allowed
Land status: State forest
Fees and permits: Vehicle pass required
Maps: State forest map; USGS Brule
Trail contacts: Brule River State Forest, 6250 South Ranger Rd., Brule, WI 54820; (715) 372-5678; dnr.wi.gov/topic/StateForests/BruleRiver

Finding the trailhead: From Brule, follow US 2 west for 2.4 miles to Clevedon Road. Turn right and head north 3.1 miles to the trailhead on the right. **Trailhead GPS:** N46 36.445' / W91 36.550'

The Hike

In the early 1800s, an explorer by the name of John Jacob Astor roamed the lands between Bayfield and Superior searching for copper for the North American Fur Company. A likely location was spotted and a mine subsequently inserted. That of course attracted attention, and dozens of other mines soon appeared, but none ever amounted to much. Around 1873, a well-to-do Englishman bought all the mines and a huge chunk of land west of the mouth of the Brule River. The land changed hands again in 1898 and went to Percival Mining Company, named after its owner James G. Percival. Traces of the Percival mine, including the shaft and miners' quarters, and a few others remain along this historic hiking trail.

The focus of the trail's past, however, is a road, the first one between Bayfield and Superior, built in 1870 and used extensively to move mail, freight, and passengers. The railroad eventually came along and displaced the road, but a heady air of history remains on this fun little trail. The entirety of this trail is densely wooded, starting with some wet, grassy sections traversed by boardwalk. About a half mile in, the Copper Range Spur takes off to the east and its namesake campground. A pair of taverns with accommodations for travelers and horses once stood at the Brule River crossing. This was the layover stop on the two-day journey, often much longer in winter when people made the trip in horse-drawn sleighs.

Just past the fork, the trail heads up a short hill. To the north is the Percival mine site, dug with steam-driven drills to a reported depth of 90 feet. Shortly past the mine, the trail crosses a wooden bridge over an unnamed creek flowing into Percival

Boardwalk through shady woods

Creek. Past the creek, an old foundation on the left (reclaimed by the forest) is that of a miner's bunkhouse, and then the trail ramps up a moderate grade to the top of Sugar Camp Hill and an overlook with far-off views of sprawling forest and the distant shore of Lake Superior. Take some time to soak it all in and contemplate what's out there—black bear, timber wolves, ubiquitous white-tailed deer, and hundreds of bird species from dainty songbirds to enormous soaring raptors.

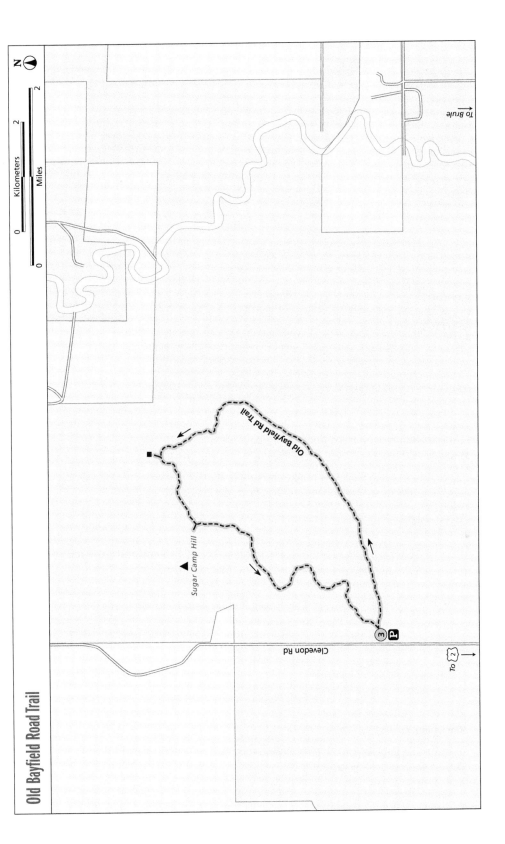

Old Bayfield Road Trail

Sugar Camp Hill

Old Bayfield Rd Trail

Clevedon Rd

3

To Brule

To 2

N

Kilometers
0   2

Miles
0   2

Faraway views north from the overlook

From the overlook, continue on a generally downhill track through a rare stand of maple and hemlock, one of the few in the entire Brule River State Forest. Pass a faded spur trail to the old fire tower and then along a few more boardwalk sections through a mix of pine and hardwood back to the trailhead.

Why Go?

The wolves are back in Wisconsin. They flourished in this area since the last of the glaciers melted, numbering around 5,000 and gracing the nights with their haunting, beautiful calls. By 1960 the last of Wisconsin's wolves were gone. But they made one of the most remarkable comebacks in the animal world, and now our state is again home to about 1,000 wolves, with a half a dozen packs living in the Brule River Valley and surrounding forest.

Miles and Directions

0.0 From the trailhead, hike northeast over the boardwalk sections.
0.5 Pass the Copper Spur Trail.
0.6 Cross the wooden bridge.
1.3 Reach the overlook at the top of Sugar Camp Hill.
2.6 Arrive back at the trailhead.

4 Tomahawk Lake Trails

Choose from three loop options in this intimate small-town park, packed with rolling hills and resplendent North Country forest. This hike earns bonus points for its trailhead access to the lake for post-hike refreshment.

Distance: 1.6 miles with options for additional miles
Difficulty: Moderate, with some hilly sections
Photogenic factor: 4
Hiking time: 45-60 minutes
Trail surface: Hard-packed dirt and grassy sections
Other trail users: None

Canine compatibility: Leashed pets allowed
Land status: Town of Barnes
Fees and permits: None
Maps: USGS Ellison Lake; town maps
Trail contacts: Town of Barnes, 3360 CR N, Barnes, WI 54983; (715) 795-2782; barnes-wi.com

Finding the trailhead: From the Barnes Town Hall, follow Barnes Road north 0.5 mile to Ellison Lake Road and turn left. Go 0.5 mile to Moore Road and turn right (north). Follow Moore Road 1.2 miles to Park Road and turn left into the park. The trail starts adjacent to the shelter and boat launch. **Trailhead GPS:** N46 36.693' / W91 51.181'

The Hike

In the late 1800s early settlers to northern Wisconsin began staking claims to new places to call home. George Barnes was among them, and he fancied the area around today's Eau Claire Lakes. Ol' George was a wise fella because this is indeed a very special place.

At the time of George's arrival, this was for the most part unsettled, wild country, populated mainly by scattered Chippewa families and a woodsman or three. The land was blanketed with dense, old-growth forest and packed with all manner of wild critters, but Mr. Barnes took to the place and settled with his family on Island Lake. In 1905, George created the Town of Barnes, consisting of a post office, saloon, grocery store, and living quarters.

His vision proved clear, and before long new settlers wandered in, eventually forming a little town that took on its founder's name. In addition to his work running the town's main establishments, George was also the postmaster and mail carrier, traveling from Barnes to Iron River with a team of horses and a carriage to retrieve his town's mail for delivery.

Since those days of discovery, challenge, and inspiration, a majority of Wisconsin's north transformed into a wildly popular summer travel destination with vividly clear lakes, loon song, and an unspoken connection to people's souls. Indeed, I share a kinship with this area's earliest residents with five generations of family heritage, and we are fiercely proud to be here.

Quiet trails in a northern forest

The Eau Claire Chain is composed of three big lakes orbited by a supporting cast of smaller ones with their own magic. The Upper, Middle, and Lower Eau Claire Lakes and friends host the headwaters of the Eau Claire River, which ambles leisurely to the St. Croix River and then south to the Mississippi.

Just north of the big three lakes is Tomahawk Lake, about 130 acres shaped like its name and home to largemouth bass, panfish, and walleye. The little town park at the lake's north end is a base camp of sorts for outdoor pursuits and a source of community pride. Among stands of elegant forest are about 5 miles of squiggly trails. An interpretive trail, with accompanying signage, is in the works. Trees harvested for additional trail expansion are used for fish habitat in the lake as well as for the fishing pier.

Start this hike traveling north from the trailhead, shortly passing the perch of the sledding hill.

GIMMER SHELTER

Snow lovers come hither! Those of the cross-country ski, snowshoe, and sledding mind will love the convenient base camp where a year-round park shelter does duty as a warming hut, changing building, and safety shelter. The location is also available for community events and offers an outdoor well with fresh, icy-cold water in warm months and comfy heat from a wood fire when the snow falls.

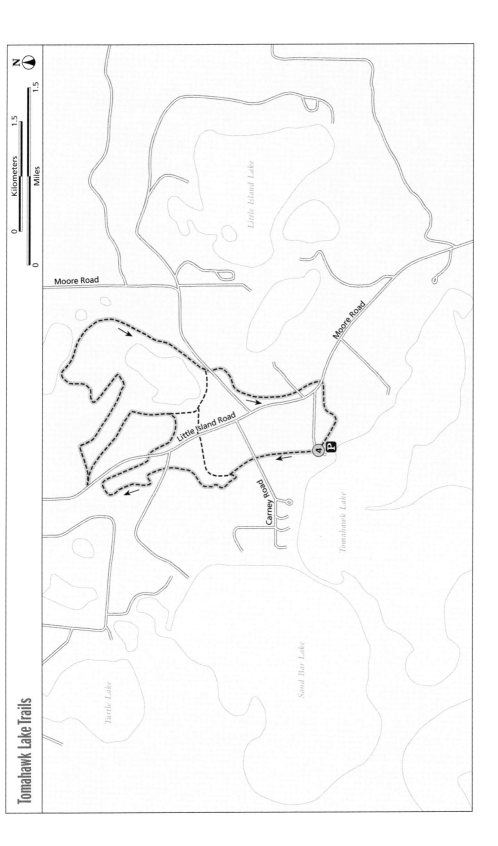

Tomahawk Lake Trails

Little Island Lake

Moore Road

Moore Road

Little Island Road

Carney Road

Tomahawk Lake

Sand Bar Lake

Turtle Lake

N

Kilometers
0   1.5

Miles
0   1.5

Trail junction rest stop

Insider's tip: Don't miss this spot for whoop-it-up fun in the winter. Bring the kids and sleds and let 'em rip.

The trail is constructed wide for skiing and the tread is largely grassy, with streaks of dirt singletrack now and again. The entire first half of this loop takes in some of the prettiest of the woods, vibrant with oak, maple, red and white pine, and some Norway pine. You'll enjoy flowing hills of varying steepness to keep things interesting, and on the eastern, back side of the loop, the terrain levels a bit on its homestretch back to the trailhead.

Huge bonus in warmer weather: a lovely little swimming beach conveniently located at trail's end for a refreshing conclusion to the hike.

Why Go?

This area is all about diversity. The forest is a rich mix of pine and hardwood blanketed over lumpy terrain perfectly suited for all manner of outdoor pursuits. Hikers, skiers, and mountain bikers all enjoy exhilarating descents (and tough workouts going back up!) on marked trails. Come out in winter and zing down the big sledding hill.

Miles and Directions

0.0 Follow the blazes and signage north from the trailhead.

0.2 Turn left at this junction.

0.9 Turn right for the short loop. (A left turn leads to the two longer loop options.) Follow this section of the trail east about 600 feet.

1.0 Turn right, hiking southbound.

1.6 Arrive back at the trailhead.

The wide, grassy trail

5 Hayward Recreational Forest

Hayward buzzes with all manner of activity in the summer months, but you can get wilderness-like peace and quiet in the town's namesake getaway forest.

Distance: 2.8 miles
Difficulty: Easy to moderate
Photogenic factor: 4
Hiking time: About 1 hour
Trail surface: Short section of gravel at start, then mowed grass
Other trail users: None

Canine compatibility: Leashed pets allowed
Land status: Town of Hayward
Fees and permits: None
Maps: USGS Stanberry East
Trail contacts: Hayward Lakes Visitors & Convention Bureau, 15805 US 63, Hayward, WI 55843; (715) 634-4801; haywardlakes.com

Finding the trailhead: From US 63 at the south side of Hayward, follow Greenwood Lane north 0.8 mile to County Hill Road. Turn left and follow County Hill west for 1.8 miles to the forest area entrance. The entrance to the forest is the first driveway past the gravel pit. Only one little sign currently stands and faces west so remember to turn after the gravel pit. **Trailhead GPS:** N46 01 078' / W91 53.476'

The Hike

Opened for business in 2011, this relatively young outdoor recreation area boasts 160 acres of mildly undulating to hilly terrain overlaid with a dense population of white and red pine, oak, maple, aspen, birch, and a variety of other species I couldn't identify. The understory is a cavalcade of shrubbery and ferns common to the north, as well as a bazillion wood ticks. The paths are mowed but be aware and check thoroughly after the hike for those little buggers.

Did I mention mosquitoes? Stop moving for more than, say, 15 seconds and they will eat you. Dry periods are typically better (less perilous) but expect the hordes all summer and bring bug repellent and appropriate clothing. I brought neither the day I hiked here and, well, I hiked fast. One other nugget to remember is the forest is closed to hiking during the annual gun deer-hunting season, from the Saturday before Thanksgiving to the Sunday after.

Okay, let's hike. The trails were designed for cross-country skiing and hence are very wide. They offer plenty of room to walk hand in hand or chase your lively child around. The first stretch of trail leading to the south parking area and warming house is on gravel, but the remaining mileage is all mowed grass. This trail system is made of a collection of loops and ancillary trails for whatever suits your mood. Today, shoot for the start of the Green Trail at the southeastern corner. This section tracks through plenty o' pines and the deciduous species mentioned above. The path undulates a little, with one gradual rise and a short, punchy climb. Pass by stands of aspen and

The wide-open forest trail (left); trail junction signs ease directional angst (right)

birch to the orange trail and head southwest to Konieczny Lake, named for the area's original landowners.

I chose this hike for its easy access from town, scenic factor, and this little, hidden lake. The lake isn't a calendar-shot candidate, but it's one of those way-out-there, all-natural places we love so much in these parts of the state. Lily pads carpet some areas of the surface and in late summer bloom with the white accents of their puffball flowers. Ancient deadfall logs float here and there, and there is almost always some form of wildlife visiting the lake. Look for ducks, herons, deer, turtles, and mosquitoes. A bench perched on the shore is great for reflection time in the fall when the bugs are gone.

The top part of the loop heads arrow-straight back to the final stretch north to the trailhead. Don't forget to come back in winter for sublime cross-country skiing and snowshoeing.

Why Go?

Wisconsin is loaded with ecological gems and one of the most fascinating is the Kissick Alkaline Bog State Natural Area. This area features a 10-acre wilderness lake surrounded by an enormous and rare quaking bog mat and wet forest. This special place

A typical crowded day on the trails

is home to no fewer than fourteen native orchid species, narrow-leaf sundew, pitcher plant, boreal sedge, and bog-rosemary. Black spruce and tamarack forest dominates the fringe of the bog, along with white cedar and cattails. The alkaline-to-acid variation inspires the bog's incredible diversity.

Miles and Directions

0.0 Head south from the trailhead and follow the green trail to the left.

0.8 Keep heading straight on the yellow trail.

1.3 Turn left on the blue trail.

1.5 Turn left on the orange trail.

2.0 Veer left/straight on the blue trail.

2.8 Arrive back at the trailhead.

Hayward Recreational Forest

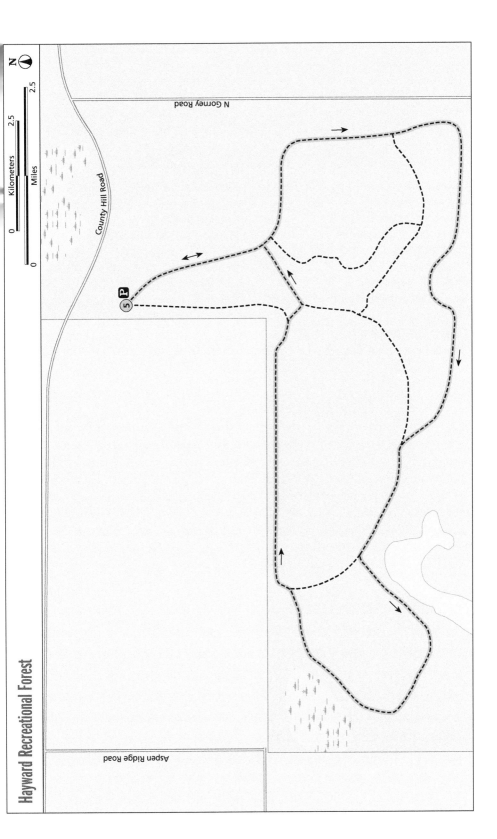

N

Kilometers
0   2.5   2.5

Miles
0   2.5

County Hill Road

N Gorney Road

Aspen Ridge Road

P

5

6 Forest Lodge Nature Trail

This trail channels its inner Oregon with dense, shady undergrowth, towering second-growth pine and hemlock, and old logs draped in emerald-green moss. Don't miss the long boardwalk into a rare and vibrant northern tamarack bog.

Distance: 1.2 miles
Difficulty: Easy
Photogenic factor: 4
Hiking time: 30–40 minutes
Trail surface: Packed dirt and spongy pine needles
Other trail users: None
Canine compatibility: Leashed pets allowed

Land status: Chequamegon-Nicolet National Forest
Fees and permits: None
Maps: Nature trail map; USGS Namekagon Lake
Trail contacts: Cable Natural History Museum, 13470 Highway M, Cable, WI 54821; (715) 798-3890; cablemuseum.org

Finding the trailhead: From Cable, follow Highway M east 8.5 miles to Garmisch Road. Turn left, and trailhead parking is 1 mile on the right. **Trailhead GPS:** N46 12.036' / W91 06.233'

The Hike

Many of the hikes in this book are in places that would be inaccessible (or wouldn't be here at all) if not for the farsighted vision of very special people. The Forest Lodge Nature Trail is one of those places and the vision started with the late Mary Griggs Burke, founder of today's Cable Natural History Museum and renowned art collector. Born to a family of considerable means, Burke's childhood and ultimate outlook on life were influenced by the forests and lakes of Wisconsin's north. Her grandfather bequeathed Forest Lodge, a sprawling property and lodge on the southern shore of Lake Namekagon, which eventually became a nearly 900-acre family compound hidden in the North Country's gentle embrace.

FRESHWATER INNOVATION

One of Wisconsin's top ten water-related academic programs, the Mary Griggs Burke Center for Freshwater Innovation is a leader in studying and advocating for health and sustainable uses of fresh water around the world. We take it for granted, but water is life to us all and we must treat it with critical care. The Burke Center conducts critical research and communication along with engaging thoughtful leadership to drive change with the public, non-governmental organizations (NGOs), and private-sector industry. The center blends its resources with Northland College to inspire water resource training and water resource solutions.

The pine-needle trail into the woods

The author on the loop trail

All grown up, Burke continued with regular retreats to the property and found time to establish the Cable Natural History Museum. In 1968 she helped create 4 miles of hiking trails near her lodge. Thirty years later, she transferred the property to the Chequamegon-Nicollet National Forest with a shared goal of research, education, and outdoor recreation. In fact, the land today is part of Northland College's Forest Lodge Educational Campus and all manner of innovative and dedicated conservation efforts.

One step onto this path and you'll know why it is hailed as one of our state's best interpretive trails, made up of three enticing loop options—the namesake Forest Lodge Nature Trail, Extended Nature Trail, and Conservancy Trail, all wandering through mesmerizing forests of hemlock, pine, birch, aspen, maple, and other hardwoods. The trail first starts near a small, grassy meadow surrounded by dense stands of white pine. You might see blackberries growing nearby as well and a short way into the woods is a huge white pine snag, a favorite stop for woodpeckers (evident from the tree's perforations) owls, flying squirrels, bats, and other birds that forage for meals here and build nests in the excavated cavities.

Look into the woods to see decaying stumps of 6- by 200-foot white pines that ruled these woods before the ax fell. You'll also see flat patches of faded green lichen attached to trees along the trail as well as funky looking old man's beard hanging from branches.

Evidence of Wisconsin's glaciated past is evident with every fascinating step. Think back about 100,000 years when unfathomably huge ice sheets crept south from Canada, scouring the earth and breaking solid bedrock into millions of pieces, carrying it along like an icy conveyor belt and dropping it somewhere else. About halfway through this hike you'll reach the boardwalk that stretches out into the bog.

Forest Lodge Nature Trail

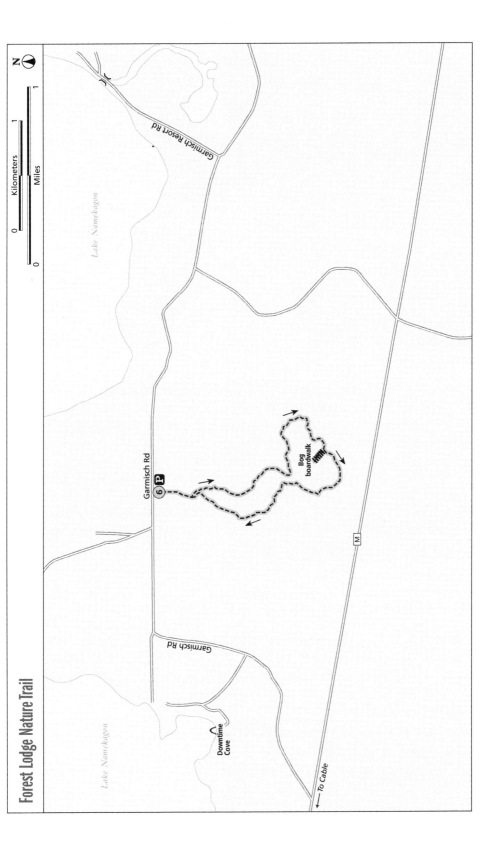

Bog boardwalk

Look left for long-stemmed cinnamon ferns and wild calla. Sphagnum moss covers the entire area like a spongy carpet. The bog also hosts insect-eating plants such as sundew and pitcher plants that trap bugs and break them down with special enzymes. Yum! In the animal world, you're likely to see, or at least hear, warblers, chickadees, and perhaps a thrush. Toads and frogs are common accompaniments as well.

A short way past the bog, the trail passes through a grove of resplendent hemlocks. Note the thick bark of the older of these handsome trees, many of which began life in downed logs or stumps. You will also see stands of balsam fir, the air full of their refreshing scent. At ground level, you'll find a variety of woodland ferns, spring ephemerals (in May and early June), and wintergreen.

Why Go?

The soul of Forest Lodge is based in environmental leadership and research in sustainability efforts, and a strong connection to the land. To that end, Northland College works closely with Special Management Areas (SMAs) that encourage the protection and responsible use of extraordinary places such as this. Management of SMAs is conducted with environmental preservation at the fore.

Miles and Directions

0.0 From the trailhead, walk through a tunnel of pines and past the small meadow.

0.6 Arrive at the bog boardwalk.

1.2 Arrive back at the trailhead.

7 Hildebrand Lake Trail

This wonderfully squiggly trail delves deep into a classic Northwoods pine-hardwood forest, with just the right blend of boulders and roots strewn about the path and great views of two remote lakes.

Distance: 3.5 miles
Difficulty: Moderate
Photogenic factor: 4
Hiking time: 1 hour
Trail surface: Hard-packed dirt, rocks, roots
Other trail users: Mountain bikes
Canine compatibility: Leashed pets allowed

Land status: Chequamegon-Nicolet National Forest
Fees and permits: None
Maps: CAMBA trail maps; USGS Lake Tahkodah
Trail contacts: Chequamegon-Nicolet National Forest, 500 Hansen Rd., Rhinelander, WI 54501; (715) 362-1300; fs.usda.gov/cnnf

Finding the trailhead: From Cable, drive 7.9 miles east on Highway M to Rock Lake Road (FR 207). Turn right (south) and head 3.2 miles to the parking area on the left. **Trailhead GPS:** N46 09 484' / W91 08 535'

The Hike

This hike is close to the previous chapter's Glacier Trail but it deserves high ranking as well, especially with the presence of a trio of way-out-there lakes lassoed by the path. I will issue another warning here about mosquitoes—the woods are full of them in summer and this trail takes you to what surely must be their main breeding grounds. I hiked here in late June and am still recovering from the trauma of impending blood-sucking doom. Early-morning hikes are somewhat of a defense, when skeeters are less amped up for human visitors, but wandering into their lair is always a gamble. Prepare accordingly with plenty of bug repellant and clothing that covers vulnerable skin.

Scary stories aside, this trail easily ranks as one of my favorites in what is argu-ably Wisconsin's most remote lands, filled to the brim with noble forest and fairy-tale terrain littered with kettles, boulders, and moss-covered logs. The Chequamegon Area Mountain Bike Association (CAMBA) will tell you this is the most technically challenging trail in their entire system; great fun for fat-tire adrenaline junkies that translates to the stuff of dreams for hikers. Short, punchy hills appear all along the trail, providing additional flavor in seemingly all the right places, but the route's overall elevation profile looks like a flat-lined heart monitor. That means you can enjoy every step of this gem without danger of quad-busting climbs.

Just over 1 mile in, after crossing the Rock Lake Trail, the path drops down a barely-there descent to the northwest shore of Frels Lake, with intermittent views through the trees. After a relaxed hairpin turn you'll arrive at No Hands Bridge, a

Rock gardens adorn the trail

renowned trail highlight. The "bridge" is a skinny boardwalk crossing of a little stream flowing from Hildebrand Lake. And I mean skinny—18 inches wide right at the surface of the water, with no handrails. It's easy enough to walk across but traversing on a bike is a whole different challenge. I love mountain biking as well but put on the brakes when faced with something like this. Cheers to those of you with the skill to shinny over this obstacle, and doubly so to those brave enough to try the optional, even skinnier (6 inches wide!) line. The penalty for inattention or riding above your pay grade? A very wet fall into the stream.

This bridge is a fun perk of the hike, however, and from here the path traces the west and south shores of the lake, with great views along the way. Hildebrand is only about 15 acres, averages around 12 feet deep, and is stomping grounds to panfish, largemouth bass, and northern pike. Enjoy a couple of rolling stretches as the trail turns back northeast, crosses the ski trail again, and cruises up a nearly imperceptible rise back to the trailhead.

THE BIRKIE

In 1973, thirty-five intrepid cross-country skiers took off from Hayward in the first American Birkebeiner race. From then, the Birkie rapidly grew into America's most prestigious cross-country ski competition, with accompanying events held year-round that attract well over 100,000 visitors and racers to the area. The race is named after Norwegian soldiers called "birkebeiners" for their birch-bark leggings.

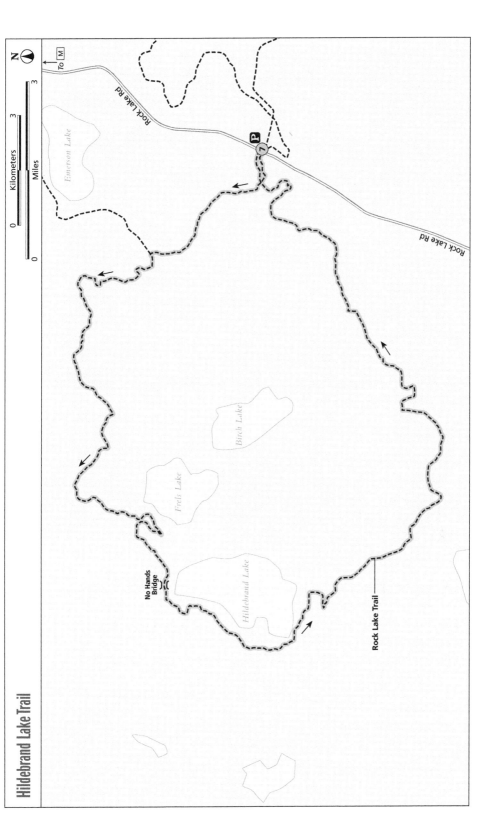

Hildebrand Lake Trail

N

To M

Kilometers
0   3

Miles
0   3

Rock Lake Rd

Emerson Lake

P
7

Rock Lake Rd

Birch Lake

Frels Lake

Hildebrand Lake

No Hands Bridge

Rock Lake Trail

Heading toward No Hands Bridge

Why Go?

If for no other reason, this trail allows us the privilege of immersing in and connecting with some of Wisconsin's finest and most remote places. Access is easy from Rock Lake Road and the trail takes hikers and bikers past the shores of wild and secluded lakes. The forest as a whole also includes rare plants such as bearberry and bloodroot, fens and bogs, and scattered stands of old-growth white pine.

Miles and Directions

0.0 Head off from the trailhead and veer right at the first fork, following the Emerson Lake Cutoff.

0.4 Go left at the Rock Lake Trail.

1.3 Meet the shore of Frels Lake.

1.6 Arrive at No Hands Bridge. Cross carefully and follow the western and southern shores of Hildebrand Lake.

2.8 Cross the Rock Lake Trail again and follow generally alongside its course back to the trailhead.

3.5 Arrive back at the trailhead.

8 Porcupine Lake Wilderness

Make a loop with the North Country Trail on this short hike in the Porcupine Lake Wilderness and score a life-list campsite for an optional overnighter.

Distance: 3 miles, with options for additional miles
Difficulty: Easy to moderate
Photogenic factor: 5
Hiking time: About 90 minutes
Trail surface: Hard-packed dirt path with scattered rocks and roots
Other trail users: None

Canine compatibility: Leashed pets allowed
Land status: National Park Service
Fees and permits: None
Maps: North Country Trail maps; USGS Diamond Lake
Trail contacts: North Country Trail Association, 229 E. Main St., Lowell, MI 49331; (866) HIKE-NCT; northcountrytrail.org

Finding the trailhead: From US 63 in Drummond, follow North Lake Owen Drive south for 5.3 miles to Porcupine Lake Road and turn left. Head east 1.3 miles to the trailhead. **Trailhead GPS:** N46 29.645' / W91 15.917'

The Hike

I like wandering in this part of the Porcupine Lake Wilderness. The North Country Trail (NCT) is extra squiggly, it's all kinds of remote out here, and the Porky is home to a wolf pack just like its wilderness neighbor to the north (Rainbow Lake). Keep an eye out for their tracks on the trails, especially in winter—there's something very special about knowing you're not alone out here.

But it feels alone, and that's a good thing. From the Porcupine Lake area, the NCT takes hikers on a many-mile stretch through some of Wisconsin's most remote lands, passing through forest packed with the likes of maple, birch, aspen, pine, hemlock, and cedar. If you're of fishing mind, Porcupine Lake teems with panfish, bluegills, and trout.

Let's talk about the NCT again for a moment. A linear trail, it takes you one way or the other, and every time I'm out here, the same thing happens—I can't decide which way to go. It's beautiful in front of me and enchanting behind. What to do? The NCT is a highlight reel of life-list hiking, and its trailheads are like a conundrum of magnetic poles luring our boots in opposite directions of wilderness grace. It's okay, though, because we win either way, and this particular loop helps out by incorporating a loop with the NCT's traditional forward progress.

Porcupine Lake Wilderness was designated as such in 1984 and is known today for its resident timber wolf pack. As I mentioned earlier in the book, wolves were vilified and killed off by, what else, human meddling. Thanks to bounties and other despicable means, their numbers plummeted to just 200 in the 1920s. The last documented wolf was hit by a car in 1958, and with that one sickening blow of a fender, they were gone.

Porcupine Creek

A scattering of holdouts held ground in neighboring Minnesota, at the time the only established population in the US outside of Alaska. But in the early to mid-1970s, wolves began to reappear in Wisconsin. There was no complex, expensive, controversial reintroduction event—the wolves simply walked back in to reclaim their place. It happened slowly at first, with a random sighting one day or forest service report the next. Their population gradually increased, and today we share our lands with around 1,000 of the regal beasts. I for one am eternally grateful; the redolent wail of their call echoing in the woods on a coal-black night is the purest of song.

Start this loop at the wilderness trailhead along Porcupine Lake Road. Walk into the woods and hike south along Porcupine Creek, a gorgeous little stream flowing clear and clean from its namesake lake out toward Lake Superior. At the junction with the NCT proper, take a left for a quick side trip to great views of the lake and then backtrack to the junction.

THE LONG WALK

Long-distance hikers are a unique breed, wearing out the soles of their boots like long-haul Peterbilts shedding tread on a sunbaked Arizona interstate. The endurance crowd can channel their inner trucker on the North Country National Scenic Trail, covering seven states and 4,600 miles. Established in 1980, with origins long before, the NCT is the country's longest continuous trail, passing through daydream-worthy scenery all the while. The trail is named for the natural splendor of Wisconsin's Chequamegon-Nicolet National Forest.

Porcupine Lake Wilderness

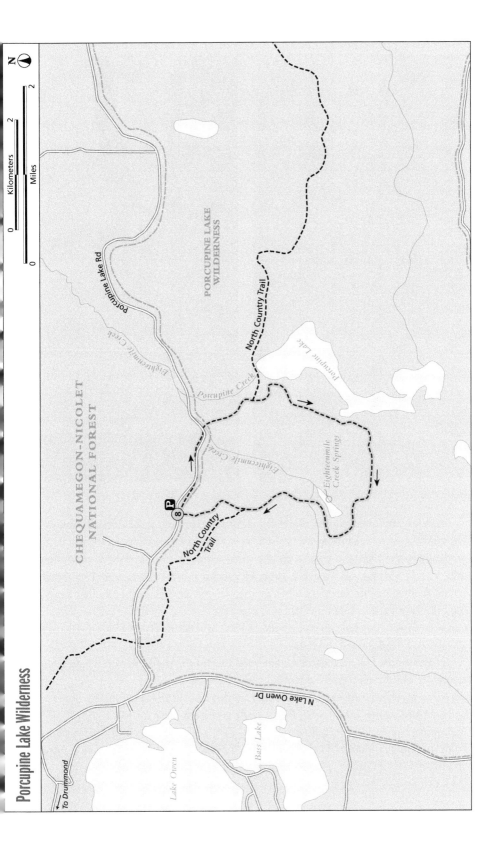

N

Kilometers
0   2

Miles
0   2

Porcupine Lake Rd

Eighteenmile Creek

CHEQUAMEGON-NICOLET
NATIONAL FOREST

Porcupine Creek

PORCUPINE LAKE
WILDERNESS

North Country Trail

Porcupine Lake

Eighteenmile Creek

Eighteenmile
Creek Springs

North Country
Trail

P
8

N Lake Owen Dr

Lake Owen

Bass Lake

To Drummond

Early trail section through the pines (left); a shoreline birch on a perfect spring day (right)

Back on the main course, the trail gently rolls through resplendent forest, offering views now and again of Porcupine Lake to the east. In a short while you'll curve gradually to the west and up to a ridgeline flanking the southern shore of Eighteenmile Creek Springs, in essence a large, elongated pond feeding into Eighteenmile Creek. A short descent drops to a bridge over the creek, and after a couple of easygoing hills through stands of pine, you will meet the junction with the spur trail heading north to Porcupine Lake Road, while the NCT continues westbound. Turn right (north) and head toward the road.

At Porcupine Lake Road turn right back toward the trailhead. You'll have to hoof it just shy of 0.5 mile, but it's downhill on soft gravel.

Want more miles? Switch it up and start this hike at the spur trail turnout/trailhead on Porcupine Lake Road. Hike south and loop back up to the north side of Porcupine Lake and then follow the NCT into a 4-mile stretch of heartbeat-quiet wilderness to the County D trailhead. Have a buddy pick you up or make a day of it and hike back to Porky's splendiferous lakeside campsites to spend the night.

Why Go?

This hike shares land with the Eighteenmile Creek State Natural Area, featuring a shaded cliff ecosystem above Eighteenmile Creek at its headwaters, rising in steps from 10 to more than 50 feet. The headwaters area also hosts a large stand of mature hemlock forest as well as pockets of its old-growth ancestors. Porcupine Lake Wilderness as a whole includes many lakes surrounded by a dense canopy of maple, yellow birch, and white and red pine. Best of all, this area has largely recovered much of its original glory after being savaged by logging, allowing us the opportunity to see the forest as it used to be.

Miles and Directions

0.0 From the trailhead, hike southbound on the generally flat trail through the woods.

0.3 Reach the junction with the NCT proper, go left to a gradual climb to a ridge with intermittent views of Porcupine Lake through the trees. ***Trail note:*** Do not miss the 0.3-mile side trip to the north end of the lake and the best views of the entire loop. Just go left at this junction to the shore and then back to finish the loop.

1.4 Follow the trail to the top of a high ridge above Eighteenmile Creek Springs.

1.8 Cross Eighteenmile Creek.

2.2 Arrive at the junction with the spur trail north, turn right.

2.5 Reach the junction with Porcupine Lake Road. Turn right and follow the dirt road back to the trailhead.

3.0 Arrive back at the trailhead.

Log bridge crossing Porcupine Creek

9 Copper Falls State Park

Score a waterfall twofer and otherworldly North Country scenery on this life-list hike in the midst of deep river gorges, lively rivers, and stately forest.

Distance: 2.3 miles (including optional side trip to the observation tower)
Difficulty: Easy to moderate
Photogenic factor: 5
Hiking time: About 90 minutes
Trail surface: Hard-packed dirt path with scattered rocks and roots
Other trail users: None
Canine compatibility: Leashed pets allowed

Land status: State park
Fees and permits: Vehicle pass required
Maps: State park maps; USGS Mellen, USGS High Bridge
Trail contacts: Copper Falls State Park, 36764 Copper Falls Rd., Mellen, WI 54546; (715) 274-5123; dnr.wi.gov/topic/parks/name/copperfalls

Finding the trailhead: From Mellen, follow WI 13 north 0.5 mile to WI 169 and continue 1.7 miles to the park entrance. Follow the park road to the picnic area parking area and trailhead. **Trailhead GPS:** N46 37.134' / W90 64.311'

The Hike

The Alps of Wisconsin? Yep, 500 to 600 million years ago (give or take a few), this was the place to be for world-class mountaineering and gnarly skiing. The 80-mile-long Penokee Range (also called by its Ojibwe name, Gogebic Range) is one of the world's oldest, predating animal life on land. These hills once soared above 10,000 feet, with snow-covered summits and deep, verdant valleys. The ridges of the Penokee are still among the highest in Wisconsin, rising more than 800 feet above Lake Superior's surface.

Two hundred million years of erosion sculpted what we see today, accompanied by glacial artistry that left behind a handful of lakes and spruce-tamarack bogs. This is a very special place indeed, filled with rich forests of birch, aspen, and maple mingling with balsam fir, white pine, cedar, spruce, tamarack, and cedar. Bogs and grasslands border the higher hills, and animal life like you saw in the wilderness areas to the west settle here in abundance.

The late 1800s attracted thousands of immigrants to the range's rich veins of iron ore. Finnish, Austrian, Swedish, French-Canadian, and other families swarmed into the area and created small towns and communities. Mined iron was shipped by rail from here to Ashland and then on to shipping freighters bound for other Great Lakes ports. The boom continued into the 1920s and this area provided much of the nation's iron until the Great Depression put a damper on things. All told, roughly 325 million tons of iron ore were extracted via very deep underground shaft mines.

Brownstone Falls

Crossing the river

After recovering from the ravages of mining, the state's noble old-growth forests were then subjected to rampant clear-cutting. The land once again recovered, and today the Penokee Range hosts a vibrant outdoors-focused tourism industry that includes hunting and fishing, mountain biking, snowmobiling, and, of course, hiking.

This hike is another of my go-to favorites for adventure and breathtaking scenery, with two calendar-shot waterfalls way down in deep, rocky gorges on an exhilarating loop trail. North Country rugged mixed with old-time charm fills the air every step of the way. The picnic area and main grounds near the trailhead are dotted with log buildings masterfully created by Civilian Conservation Corps members in the 1930s, surrounded by rich forests of hemlock, pine, sugar maple, birch, and basswood. Within the woods are dozens of wildlife species including tiger swallowtail butterflies, frogs, deer, pileated woodpeckers, and loons.

The history of this special place is equally intriguing and evident all along the hike in a fascinating blend of geologic artistry and copper-mining tradition. After enormous flows of lava oozed from the earth, and layer upon layer of various types of rock formed on the land, the Bad River was born and has spent the past untold millions of years carving its way toward Lake Superior. Today we are treated to the result of the river's efforts in the 100-foot-deep gorge of Brownstone Falls.

Copper Falls State Park

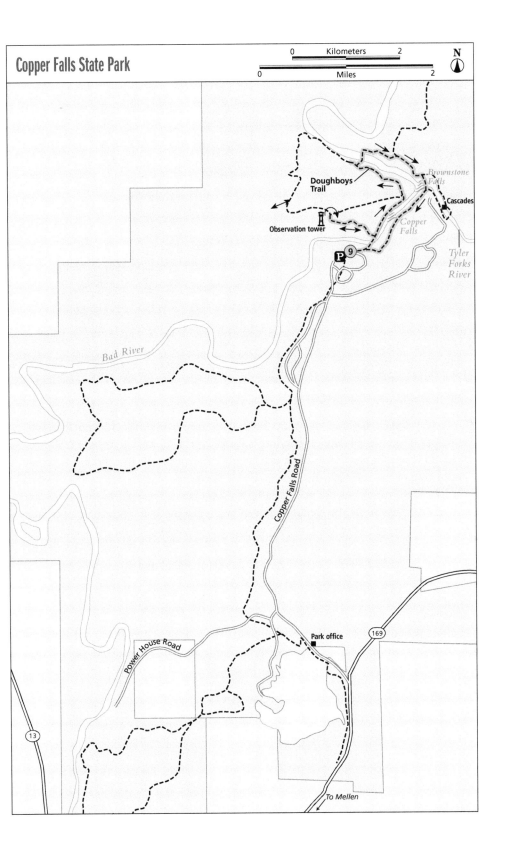

Kilometers 0 — 2
Miles 0 — 2

N

Doughboys
Trail

Brownstone
Falls

Cascades

Observation tower

Copper
Falls

P 9

Tyler
Forks
River

Bad River

Copper Falls Road

Power House Road

Park office

169

13

To Mellen

Admiring Copper Falls from an overlook

A very long time after the gorge took shape, early American Indians followed receding glaciers north, and later tribes, called Copper Culture Indians, established areas of copper mining. European settlers made valiant attempts to continue the pursuit of copper but had little success.

Start this fun hike at the parking area and immediately cross a short footbridge over the Bad River. At the top of a gradual rise is the junction with the trail to the observation tower to the left. Lots of stairs climb the steep ridge and a few more take you to the top of the tower for amazing views of the forest unfurling in all directions. Can you see Lake Superior way out there to the north? When you've had your fill, head back to the river junction to continue the hike.

A wide, manicured stretch of trail leads to an overlook of Copper Falls, all told dropping about 29 feet in a collection of mini waterfalls flowing over jumbles of boulders. From here, the trail rises to another overlook with stellar views of Brownstone Falls shinnying through 100 feet of sandstone and black shale. Continue hiking west along the ridge above the steep walls of Devil's Gate to a flight of stone steps descending to the river. This is a great spot to wander on sandbars and get up close to the river when water levels are low. (When the river flows tumultuous, of course, use caution.)

Follow the bridge over the river and turn eastbound, climbing back up to the top of the northern ridge and past the junction with the North Country Trail's (NCT) arrival to the park's main attractions. (Our trail shares ground with the NCT from here.) A little farther on is a short spur trail leading to yet another overlook above the river, this time with great views of the confluence of the Tyler Forks River with the Bad River, Brownstone Falls, and the Tyler Forks Cascades. Keep hiking along the river to a bridge crossing just upstream from the cascades, and loop back past a couple more overlooks on the homestretch back to the trailhead.

Why Go?

In addition to the 500-acre Copper Falls State Natural Area surrounding its namesake falls, this state park is a veritable who's who of celebrity wildlife. Fishers join white-tailed deer, and elk now live nearby. More than 200 bird species live or pass through the park, including pileated woodpeckers, bald eagles, and loons. Watch at ground level and water as well for the likes of wood turtles, snakes (non-poisonous), and swallowtail butterflies.

Miles and Directions

0.0 Set off from the trailhead and cross the bridge.

0.1 Reach the junction with the observation-tower trail on your left.

0.3 Reach the tower and climb it for the views, then retrace your tracks to the river.

0.5 Arrive back at the river, follow the trail to the Copper Falls overlook and onward up the ridge.

0.7 Reach the overlook above Brownstone Falls, follow the path west along the ridge.

0.9 Cross the bridge over the Bad River.

1.2 Reach the junction with the North Country Trail. (Doughboys Trail shares ground with the NCT from here.)

1.3 Arrive at the spur trail to river overlook.

1.5 Cross the bridge over the Tyler Forks River.

2.3 Arrive back at the trailhead.

HISTORIC PEDIGREE

In November 1935 Company D-692 of the Civilian Conservation Corps (CCC) moved into Camp Copper Falls. The 164-strong company was made of carpenters, masons, furniture makers, and blacksmiths. In the ensuing 2 years, the skilled company built the park's recreational lodge, which included a granite fireplace along with log-inspired benches and tables—and that was just the beginning. The crew also built a pump house, water reservoirs, and the soaring observation tower as well as running water and telephone lines. Some crew members were charged with clearing areas for visitor parking and picnicking, as well as creating space for camping. With ten contributing properties constructed by the CCC, Copper Falls State Park is listed on the National Register of Historic Places.

10 Big Ravine Trail

It's tough to beat hiking in the company of old-growth hemlocks and cedars with birch and balsam accompaniments, all housed in conservancy land within shouting distance of the greatest of the Great Lakes.

Distance: 2.2 miles
Difficulty: Moderate, with a short, steep climb at the end
Photogenic factor: 4
Hiking time: 50-60 minutes
Trail surface: Hard-packed dirt
Other trail users: None

Canine compatibility: Leashed pets allowed
Land status: Town of Bayfield
Fees and permits: None
Maps: City and county maps; USGS Bayfield
Trail contacts: Bayfield Regional Conservancy, 33 North 1st St., Bayfield, WI 54814; (715) 779-5263; brcland.org

Finding the trailhead: From downtown Bayfield, follow 4th Street uphill to Sweeny Avenue. Turn left and park in the lot next to the ballfield. The trail starts behind the right field fence. **Trailhead GPS:** N46 48.542' / W90 49.152'

The Hike

This hike's name alone heralds something intriguing and throws in an A-list view right from the start. The trailhead's elevation above town offers a spellbinding view of Lake Superior and Madeline Island, and there's a great chance you'll see one of the ferries chugging across to the island from Bayfield Harbor.

It's easy to imagine the wild of this place so many generations past, when Ojibwe, Ottawa, Huron, and Sioux people settled and thrived here. Bayfield's rich history is also colored with the opening of the Sault St. Marie locks, ushering in the era of big "laker" ships and port terminals transferring grain, lumber, and iron ore all over the world. Today's Bayfield is a quaint and wildly popular year-round travel destination and gateway to the revered Apostle Islands.

Sufficiently inspired, head toward the ballfield and trail map kiosk to start the hike. The path skirts the top edge of the ravine on one side and the outfield fence on the other. (I wonder if some powerful home run blasts send balls sailing into the ravine's oblivion.) The view into the ravine is intoxicating and lends a mysterious air to just what might be down there. Don't wander too close to the edge (and keep an eye on young, curious kids) lest you quite dramatically and rapidly find out.

The Big Ravine Nature Preserve is part of the Bayfield Regional Conservancy, a conservation group dedicated to preserving special lands, and we can thank their efforts for places like this. The birds and their ground-based brethren thank them too. Migratory birds are especially plentiful in May and June and join well over one hundred other resident species, including ubiquitous chickadees, grosbeaks, cardinals,

The trail along the edge of the ravine

finches, woodpeckers, and many more. The forest itself hosts elusive fox, snowshoe hare, coyote, bats, wild turkey, and lots of deer.

The trail climbs steadily but gradually through resplendent forest of aromatic cedar; various pine species; mixed hardwoods such as birch, maple, oak, and aspen; as well as pockets of regal hemlocks. Indeed, the ravine and its accompanying forest hold "extreme ecological importance" and recent acquisition of an additional 40 acres here further ensures protection of critical, unfragmented woodland habitat.

About 0.5 mile into the hike, veer right at a trail junction to the overlook loop, which in spring and fall is a great spot to take in stellar views of Lake Superior and

Purple accents among the green

Madeline Island, and, on clear days, the Porcupine Mountains far across the water. I particularly appreciate that these woods provide a living, evolving, hands-on outdoor classroom for students of the nearby Bayfield School. There's no better way to learn about the place in which we live than contact with it.

Back on the main trail, hang a right and hike southeast, eventually arriving at an open field/storage area. The path continues directly across the field and through another stretch of dense woods, past a water tank, and deposits you into the quiet neighborhood along 5th Street. I included this short additional walk because it's just

LAKE SUPERIOR ICE ROAD

It's 2 miles across Lake Superior from Bayfield to LaPointe on Madeline Island, traversed via a pleasant ferry ride when the weather is equally so. But this is northern Wisconsin. With long, cold winters and frozen water, it is no place for an open-air floating vessel. Does that mean island residents are cut off from the outside world, that visitors are left stuck in their boots on the mainland? Not a chance. The Ice Road becomes the winter tie that binds. With sufficiently thick ice, this temporary thoroughfare provides unique passage from here to there (with no stoplights or traffic jams), whether by car, foot, bicycle, or snowmobile. Some people even skate across! When the ice is too thin for vehicles, the windsled takes over—a houseboat (boatmobile?) on skis powered by two enormous fans.

Big Ravine Trail

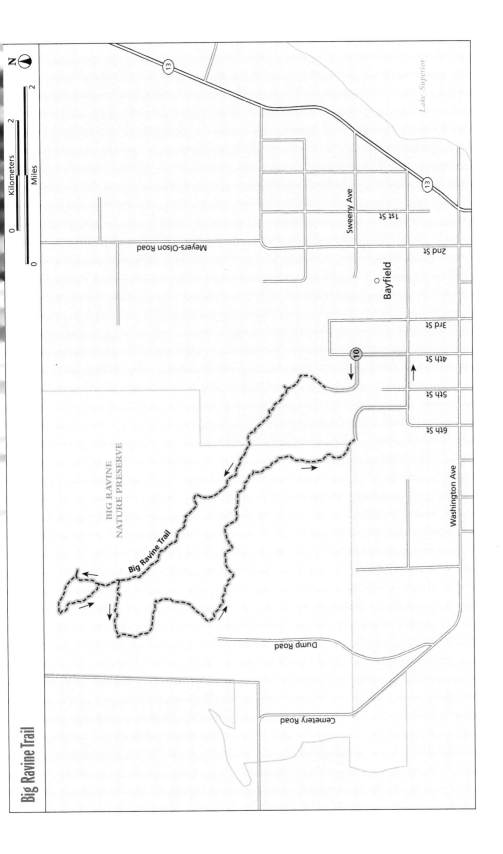

Boulder portal on the trail

plain fun to walk around Bayfield and there's a beautiful garden at one of the homes along 4th Street headed back to the parking area. There's a steep climb on Sweeny to top things off, but it's worth every step!

Why Go?

For nearly 25 years, the Bayfield Regional Conservancy has preserved more than 4,600 acres of land in Wisconsin, ensuring access to and enjoyment of exceptional places of scenic and historic value for future generations, including the likes of Frog Bay Tribal National Park, the Brownstone Trail, and Houghton Falls Nature Preserve in addition to the Big Ravine Nature Preserve.

Miles and Directions

0.0 From the trailhead, follow the trail along the ballfield fence and into the woods beyond.

0.5 Veer right at this junction and right again shortly thereafter toward the overlook. Make the overlook loop and return to the original junction.

0.8 Turn right here for the second half of the loop.

1.0 Arrive at an open field. Hike straight across to find the trail back into the woods.

1.6 Pass a big water tank.

1.8 Continue on neighborhood streets.

2.2 Arrive back at the trailhead.

11 Madeline Island–Big Bay State Park

Half the fun is getting there on this pair of hikes on the largest and most southern of Lake Superior's Apostle Islands. Hop the Madeline Island Ferry and hit up Big Bay State Park for fairy-tale lake views and the best swimming beach on the South Shore, or go remote at the island's wilderness preserve.

Distance: 3.2 miles on the point; optional 2 miles out and back on the beach boardwalk
Difficulty: Easy to moderate
Photogenic factor: 5
Hiking time: About 90 minutes for the bay loop; 45-60 minutes for the beach boardwalk
Trail surface: Hard-packed dirt and boardwalk
Other trail users: None

Canine compatibility: Leashed pets allowed on trails but not on boardwalk
Land status: State park
Fees and permits: Vehicle pass required
Maps: State park maps; USGS Ashland
Trail contacts: Big Bay State Park, 2402 Hagen Rd., La Pointe, WI 54850; (715) 747-6425; dnr.wi.gov/topic/parks/name/bigbay

Finding the trailhead: From Bayfield, board a Madeline Island Ferry or other vessel to reach the island. Once on the island in La Pointe, follow CR H east 3.8 miles to its junction with Hagen Road. Continue east on Hagen Road 2 miles to the park entrance. Find the trailhead at the day-use picnic areas. **Trailhead GPS:** N46 79.734' / W90 66.899'

The Hike

Throughout this book I write of the otherworldly power of glaciers and their impact on the Wisconsin we see today. Indeed, all corners of the state were created by the scouring of mile-high ice four times over, but what about the Apostle Islands?

We don't often relate glaciers to islands, but the Apostles are actually 600-million-year-old remnants of enormous rocks left behind by glaciers in the Lake Superior basin. And these rocks are tough, hanging in there through 100,000 years of determined glacial events. Madeline Island emerged from the fray about 15,000 years ago, only to continue its metamorphosis at the hands of waves and currents, some of which constructed today's sandy beach and lagoon at Big Bay State Park.

It's only fitting that the largest of the Apostle Islands hosts a big ol' state park to match. Big Bay State Park is 2,300 acres of amazingness, with a riveting mix of ecosystems from the sandy shore to bogs to forested ridgeline. Adjacent to the park's campground is the wonderfully unique Big Bay Sand Spit and Bog, 440 acres of floating sphagnum-sedge bog, stately second-growth boreal forest, and a vibrant population of bog flora.

On a hot summer day, Big Bay's long, sprawling beach is the place to be, with plenty of room to stretch out on a lounge chair, build a sandcastle, or paddle a kayak around the bay. The Boardwalk Trail is another don't-miss park highlight. The

Idyllic rest stop along the trail DENICE BREAUX

0.5-mile, flat trail parallels the beach on its way through an enchanting stand of red and white pines near the spit.

If you can pry away from the already lovely distractions near the bay, head for the Woods Trail for a view-packed hike along the rounded, woodsy nub above Lake Superior.

Starting from the campground area, follow Woods Trail toward the southern end of the point and hop onto Point Trail. From here the path encounters a few mild ups

HERMIT ISLAND

A couple of miles northwest of the northern tip of Madeline Island lies Hermit Island, a small oval of dense woods and low cliffs that hosted brownstone quarries from the early 1860s to 1890s. But the island is known more for its ghost than rocks. William Wilson, a resident of LaPointe on Madeline Island, lost a fistfight bet with the town's magistrate and was exiled to a nearby island. Wilson didn't mind it out there at all and made a decent living crafting barrels for the big lake ships. In the depths of winter in 1861, no smoke had been seen from Wilson's island home for a few days and a posse discovered him dead inside the house. Murder was suspected and some say Wilson didn't take kindly to that and his ghost still wanders the island today.

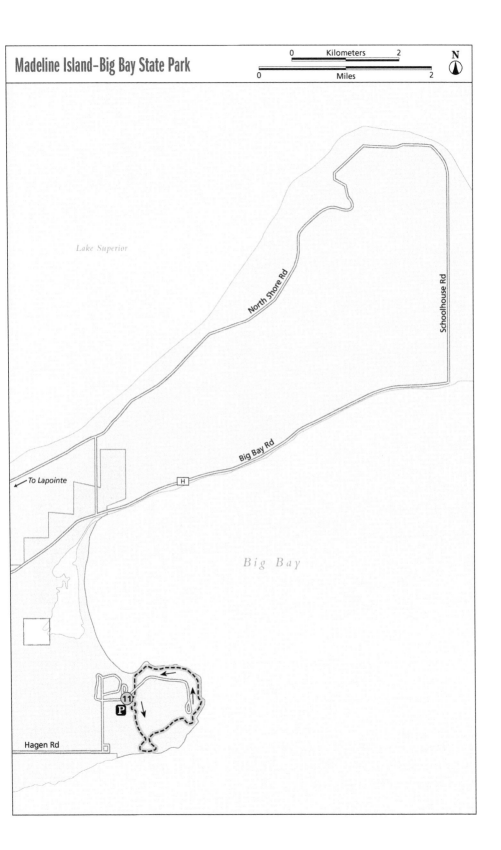

Madeline Island–Big Bay State Park

Kilometers 0 — 2

Miles 0 — 2

N

Lake Superior

North Shore Rd

Schoolhouse Rd

Big Bay Rd

H

← To Lapointe

Big Bay

11

P

Hagen Rd

Magnificent Lake Superior shoreline DENICE BREAUX

and downs in terrain as it curves along the point. You will soon merge with Bay View Trail and be treated to several overlooks with gorgeous views out over Lake Superior. A barely noticeable descent takes you back to the trailhead, where there's easy access to the don't-miss beach boardwalk trail.

The boardwalk trail is a pan-flat treat tracking arrow-straight through an aged forest of pine, aspen, birch, and maple. The beach is only steps away if you feel a spontaneous urge to jump in, and the path also leads directly to the above-mentioned Big Bay Sand Spit. Good times, indeed.

Resplendent forest on Bay View Trail DENICE BREAUX

Why Go?

Madeline Island is home to an array of extraordinary ecosystems, including high cliffs, caves, beaches, and dense, remote forest. Birds are especially keen on the island's offerings and visitors to the far north and south ends of the island, as well as Big Bay Town Park and Big Bay Lagoon, are treated to some of Wisconsin's finest birding opportunities. Spring sees the return of sandhill cranes and great blue herons, and warmer months bring the piping plover and common tern. Snowy owls and bald eagles remain common throughout winter. Like every other natural environment on earth, Madeline is changing. National and local agencies and volunteer groups continue to monitor the island's ecosystems to ensure their best possible health and well-being while staying alert for long-term threats.

Miles and Directions

0.0 From the trailhead, follow Woods Trail roughly southeast to the lakeshore and turn left on Point Trail.

1.2 Point Trail merges with Bay View Trail. Keep hiking around the point. The path leads right back to the trailhead and easy access to the optional Boardwalk Trail.

3.2 Arrive back at the trailhead.

12 Mount Ashwabay–Trogdor Trail

Wander sublime fern-lined trail in the shade of aspen and maple (a trailside forest gnome leads the way) and score linger-worthy views from the top of Mount Ashwabay.

Distance: 3.3-mile lollipop
Difficulty: Moderate to challenging
Photogenic factor: 5
Hiking time: 60–75 minutes
Trail surface: Hard-packed dirt
Other trail users: Mountain bikers
Canine compatibility: Leashed pets allowed

Land status: Chequamegon National Forest
Fees and permits: None
Maps: CAMBA maps; USGS Mount Ashwabay
Trail contacts: Chequamegon-Nicolet National Forest, 500 Hansen Rd., Rhinelander, WI 54501; (715) 362-1300; fs.usda.gov/cnnf

Finding the trailhead: From Washburn, follow WI 13 north 6.5 miles to Whiting Road and turn left. The trailhead is 1.6 miles on the right. **Trailhead GPS:** N46 46.032' / W90 54.122'

The Hike

Hiking trails come in all shapes and sizes, long and short, steep and flat, woods, mountains, desert, you name it. I've been very fortunate to set my boots down on all of those and it never fails, sooner or later someone asks, "What's your favorite trail?" Short of saying they're all favorites, I dodge the question because every path has its own vibe and drives exhilarating satisfaction into my bones in different ways. But some trails stand out and I find myself grinning in delight with every step.

This is one of those trails. Once again, Chequamegon Area Mountain Bike Association (CAMBA) created a beauty. Every inch of tread is impeccably maintained as it twists and bends through drop-dead gorgeous forest, teases with lower elevation overlooks, and then climbs to a crescendo of cover-shot views of distant valleys, Lake Superior, and Madeline Island. At the end of the hike I nearly turned around and did it again!

What's so great about this place? After all, the "mount" is not exactly Denali-like, and purveyors of skiing in the Rockies or Montana or most anywhere else in the

LET'S GO SKIING

In the 1940s (some say even earlier) Mount Ashwabay attracted a few skiers, and it didn't take long for word to spread. People traveled from all over the state to cruise and race. Today the mountain hosts twelve runs, a tubing hill, skijoring, snowshoe and cross-country ski trails, snowboard camps, and an outdoor education program packed with year-round activities. In warmer months, the area is a go-to for mountain biking and hiking. This little hill is big on tradition and remains a fan favorite.

In the company of ferns

world will scoff at Ashwabay's vertical drop. But this little hill is more than 600 million years old and filled to its modest, rounded summit with equal parts rich geologic history and proud tradition. Once buried under glacial Lake Duluth, Mount Ashwabay and its surrounding area are part the Bayfield group, a 4,300-foot-thick quartz sandstone formation. I'd wager that fact was lost on skiers clad in plaid flannel in the 1940s as they zipped down on wooden skis and cable-latched boots from Ashwabay's 1,312-foot summit.

It was lost on me, too, the day I hiked through the woods to the peak up yonder. I was simply reveling in the moment and was all kinds of grateful to be part of this special place, a feeling that flushed through me about six steps from the trailhead.

As you begin the hike, be aware that the first part of this hike, on the Hot Saw trail, goes against mountain biking traffic, so pay attention. The path immediately dives into forest crowded with everything from white pine to aspen, all vying for attention. And the ferns! The ground is fully concealed by waist-high fern fields and the path wanders right through in gently undulating squiggles. Along this stretch you'll meet a little trailside gnome statue decked out in chaps and a pointy hat as the trail dips though a shallow ravine and then starts climbing. A brief break in the trees offers a provocative view of the southern tip of Madeline Island and the Ashland breakwater.

Continue uphill to a six-way intersection that would baffle your directional savvy if not for CAMBA's reliable and accurate signage. Head to the left on Trogdor Trail. This is where the hike gets really fun, twisting in tight hairpins and tumbling over rock gardens; it seems the trail itself is having just as great a time. See if you can spot the

Doesn't get much better than this

wooden chair covered in lichen and old stories as it sits nestled in the foliage. It's a hoot following all the abrupt changes in direction and waves in the trail on the steady climb upward. Funny thing is, the hike is such a blast you hardly notice it's going uphill.

But rise it does and soon emerges at the top of Mount Ashwabay. I half expected cherubs, rays of golden light, and a hallelujah chorus—the view is the stuff of daydreams. Straight to the north the valley dips far below and swoops high again and that's where all kinds of homegrown organic farms, laced with generations-deep heritage, grow delicious berries, apples, and veggies. Don't miss a trip over that way. To the northwest is the Nourse Sugarbush State Natural Area and to the right Lake Superior and Madeline Island. This is the proverbial picture-perfect place to stretch out, watch clouds change shapes, and listen to the birds sing.

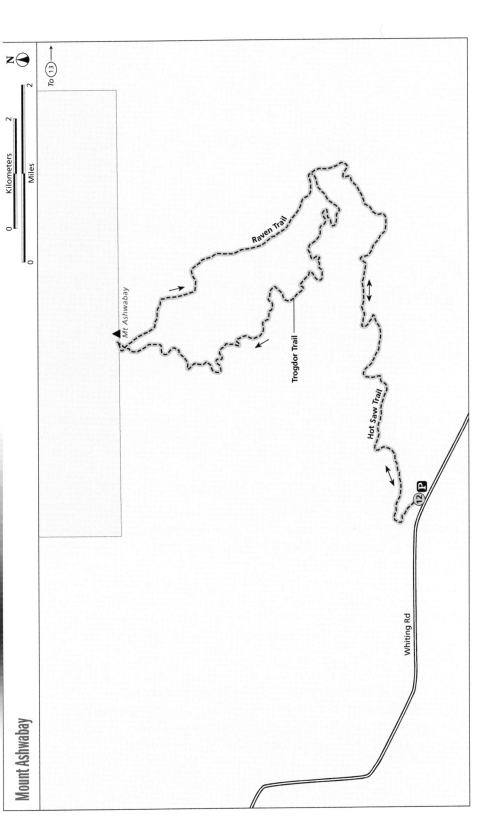

Mount Ashwabay

Raven Trail

Mt Ashwabay

Trogdor Trail

Hot Saw Trail

Whiting Rd

12 P

To 13

N

Kilometers
0   2   2

Miles
0   2

A daydream scene from the top of the mountain

Post-lounging, walk along the ridge southeast to meet the Raven Trail. This path follows a gently curving course along the hill's outer fringe back down to that crowded intersection. From here, simply retrace Hot Saw Trail back south through the ferns to the trailhead.

Why Go?

Settled in Mount Ashwabay's northwestern shadow, the Nourse Sugarbush State Natural Area is home to huge, old-growth hemlocks and 100-foot sugar maples, with an accompanying cast of birch, red oak, basswood, balsam fir, and a rich variety of groundcover. All of this makes ideal habitat for the rare black-throated blue warbler, and true to its name, the natural area also boasts maple sugaring history dating back hundreds of years. A hike through this treasured area reveals slash marks on some trees from those early days of tree tapping.

Miles and Directions

0.0 Set off from the trailhead on the Hot Saw Trail and follow it eastbound.

0.9 Reach junction with six-way conglomeration of trails; head left on the Trogdor Trail.

1.8 Arrive at the summit. Ogle the view and hike southeast to the Raven Trail for the descent.

2.3 Arrive back at the six-way intersection, continue south on Hot Saw Trail.

3.3 Arrive back at the trailhead.

13 Mount Valhalla Trails

Hike fern-lined trails in the company of showy hardwood forest in summer and return in the fall when the whole place glows in fiery autumn dress.

Distance: 2 miles, with options for additional miles
Difficulty: Moderate
Photogenic factor: 4
Hiking time: 40–45 minutes
Trail surface: Wide, grassy trail with some sections of packed dirt
Other trail users: None

Canine compatibility: Leashed pets allowed
Land status: Chequamegon-Nicolet National Forest
Fees and permits: Vehicle pass required
Maps: Forest maps; USGS Washburn
Trail contacts: Chequamegon-Nicolet National Forest, 500 Hansen Rd., Rhinelander, WI 54501; (715) 362-1300; fs.usda.gov/cnnf

Finding the trailhead: From WI 13 in Washburn, follow CR C 8.2 miles west to the parking area on the left. **Trailhead GPS:** N46 60.907' / W91 89.247'

The Hike

It can be hard to believe for folks from other parts of the country that this part regularly breeds national and Olympic champion athletes. A very short list of superstars from the Upper Midwest includes names such as Lindsey Vonn, Eric Heiden and sister Beth, Connie Carpenter-Phinney, Dan Jansen, Neal Broten, and Garry Bjorklund. One of the ingredients in the development of such otherworldly performers is challenging outdoor training in places like Mount Valhalla. This remote, heavily wooded hill has Nordic skiing in its soul and in fact served as a training base for the US Olympic team. The lumpy terrain was the ideal proving grounds and still provides a tailor-made backdrop for elite skiers and weekend cruisers as well.

Valhalla's trails are separated into the Teuton and Valkyrie clusters. This hike follows trails in the former, particularly the A and B trails. All told, there are more than

A FROLIC IN THE SNOW

The 1940 winter season started with a Snow Frolic day of cross-country skiing, alpine slalom, ski jumping, and toboggan chutes. The Queen of the Valkyries (crowned from a bevy of local contenders) held court from a "throne" sculpted from ice. All kind of records were broken on the 60-meter ski jump hill (185 feet!). Community officials and eager skiers were convinced Mount Valhalla would soon become the most popular winter destination in the Upper Midwest. Alas, Valhalla did not have motorized lifts and skiers had to walk up a long, steep stairway to reach the top.

Foliage encroachment

10 miles of trails on the Teuton system groomed for classic and skate skiing and about 11 miles on the Valkyrie side for classic only. At the trailhead, take note of the large chalet set up to accommodate winter skiers. A fireplace and portly barrel stove keep it toasty warm in there after a long day on the trails, and it's a favorite haunt for picnics and group events. All those wide, hilly trails are great fun for hiking, too, and our hike starts with a long, steady climb through dense woods. In fact, you can expect quiet, remote forest with every turn out here. Well, quiet with the exception of the portentous, high-pitched whine of mosquitoes come to welcome your day of reckoning. Fair warning for summer hikers: Bathe in bug spray before heading out here or wear adequate protective clothing (hazmat suit) to save your hide.

A few dozen steps from the trailhead, veer right onto the Loop A trail and do a little westerly curve to a four-way intersection. Go left on Loop B, continuing a persistent uphill trajectory on the wide, grassy path. Keep your eyes and ears alert for resident wild critters, including the traditional cast of frogs, squirrels, grouse, and a few wild turkey. Melodic songbirds such as warblers, wood thrush, grosbeaks, chickadees, and lots more will serenade you.

Near the junction with Loop C, lean left again to keep on Loop B, descending now. A few squiggles in the trail lead to a final straight-ahead homestretch back to the trailhead. The mosquitoes and fading daylight chased me off the hill early and turned

Mount Valhalla Trails

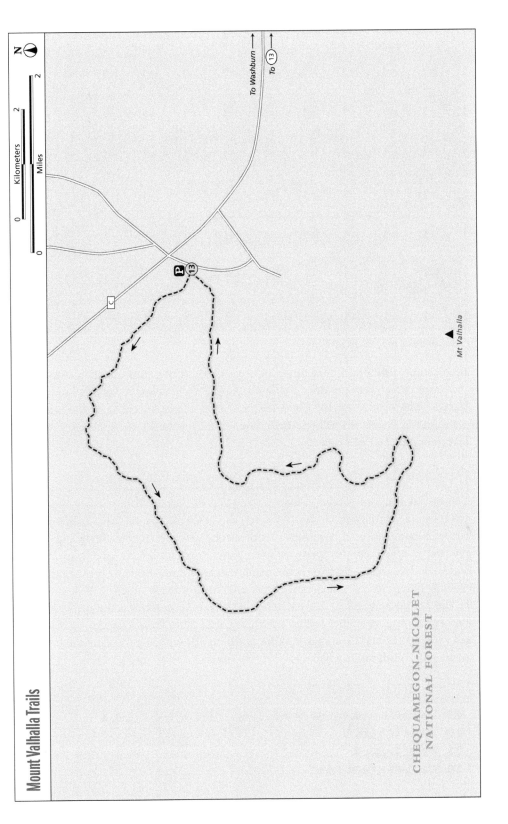

To Washburn

To 13

N

Kilometers
0   2   2

Miles
0   2

P

13

C

Mt Valhalla

CHEQUAMEGON-NICOLET
NATIONAL FOREST

Ferns dominate the forest floor

the hike into this little 2-miler, but you have all kinds of options for longer loops. One great choice is to continue uphill on Loop C to get close to Valhalla's summit (the trail shies away about 100 feet below) and make a long descent along the eastern ridge. And of course the Valkyrie trails have a full day's worth of exploring as well. Take your pick and go wander!

Why Go?

A short way south of Mount Valhalla is the Moquah Barrens State Natural Area, an extensive pine barrens (more than 600 acres) and National Natural Landmark. A pine barrens is savanna-like in appearance, with shrubs, grasses, and trees, including jack pine, red pine, and oak that thrive on fire rejuvenation. This unique place is part of a large-scale, long-term effort to restore wildlife and pollinator habitat—great news for bees and butterflies, as well as native birds and fauna of many other ilk. Wildflowers are also a focal point of the barrens, infusing vibrant color in this sandy, sparse environment. Spring welcomes barren strawberry, wild columbine, Canada mayflower, and wood anemone. In summer, look for northern plains blazing star, false sunflower, showy goldenrod, and harebell.

Miles and Directions

0.0   Hike into the woods from the chalet on the wide, grassy trail following Loop A.

0.3   Veer left onto Loop B.

0.9   Stay left for Loop B.

2.0   Arrive back at the trailhead.

14 North Lakeland Discovery Center

From young kids learning about butterflies to esteemed scientists conducting critical research, the North Lakeland Discovery Center (NLDC) is a wonderful place of learning and giving back, with relaxing and engaging hiking trails to connect with it all.

Distance: 1.2 miles, with options for additional miles
Difficulty: Easy
Photogenic factor: 4
Hiking time: About 45 minutes
Trail surface: Hard-packed dirt path and some boardwalk
Other trail users: None

Canine compatibility: Leashed pets allowed
Land status: Private
Fees and permits: None
Maps: North Lakeland Discovery Center maps; USGS Winchester
Trail contacts: North Lakeland Discovery Center, 14006 Discovery Ln., Manitowish Waters, WI 54545; (877) 543-2085; discoverycenter.net

Finding the trailhead: From the village of Manitowish Waters at US 51, follow CR W north 1.2 miles to Discovery Lane and turn left. Follow this road 0.3 mile to the center. The trails begin adjacent to the center's main building. **Trailhead GPS:** N46 14.797' / W89 89.427'

The Hike

The NLDC is the mother lode of nature-based activity, from children's outings to scientific research, all of which showcases and works to preserve this enchanting area of Wisconsin.

Young and old, casual and formal, the education center hosts the likes of youth nature groups, state wildlife and ecosystem organizations, birding and gardening clubs, and an active citizen science group taking part in Monarch tagging, wolf howl surveys, crane counts, and Christmas bird counts.

The center is a nature-based education and community gathering place encouraging responsible and enriching use of Wisconsin's Northland. Part of their mission

NORTHWOODS BIRDING FESTIVAL

The NLDC hosts a very popular birding festival every year at the center and various locations around northern Wisconsin. Held at the end of May, the event brings in esteemed speakers, authors, environmental professionals, and other notables, and field trips take place throughout. Participants enjoy hikes to places such as the Van Vliet Hemlocks, Frog Lake, and Presque Isle; photography tours; and, of course, all kinds of birding trips. Free guided nature hikes happen regularly, along with teen retreats, invasive species-identification training, investigative canoe trips, and cycling days with a naturalist.

Peaceful and calm Statehouse Lake Denice Breaux

statement rings especially true: "Enriching lives and inspiring an ethic of care for Wisconsin's Northwoods." Nice.

Among the center's programs are nature study and recreation opportunities for groups such as the Center for Conservation Leadership and the Wisconsin Land+Water Youth Conservation Camp. Groups like these are treated to an incomparable teaching and learning environment packed with lakes, forests, and bogs. The center also hosts wildly popular birding events and outings, naturalist programs, a garden club, and intensive invasive-species research and removal efforts.

The Nature Nook is a cozy destination for children of all ages and houses a stocked nature-education library, youth activities, and a rotating lineup of area critters. All manner of year-round recreation opportunities top it off. No doubt about it, this place is chock-full of outdoor goodness.

Yep, the pride in and dedication to nature is palpable here at the center and all along the hiking trails. Like this short and vibrant loop around Statehouse Lake, with a section of boardwalk through a bog and wildlife all over the place. From the trailhead, hike along the west side of the interpretive trail, paralleling the bog on your left. The boardwalk section starts at the top of the loop and is a glorious walk through a fascinating world of spongy, mossy ground; miniature ecosystems; and parades of

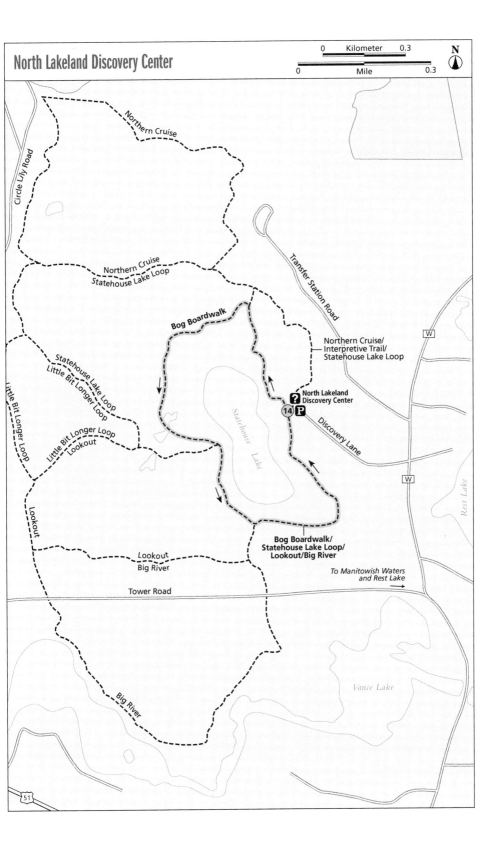

0   Kilometer   0.3

0   Mile   0.3

N

Circle Lily Road

Northern Cruise

Transfer Station Road

Northern Cruise
Statehouse Lake Loop

Bog Boardwalk

Northern Cruise/
Interpretive Trail/
Statehouse Lake Loop

W

Statehouse Lake Loop
Little Bit Longer Loop

North Lakeland
Discovery Center

14 P

Little Bit Longer Loop

Little Bit Longer Loop
Lookout

Statehouse Lake

Discovery Lane

W

Rest Lake

Lookout

Bog Boardwalk/
Statehouse Lake Loop/
Lookout/Big River

Lookout
Big River

To Manitowish Waters
and Rest Lake

Tower Road

Big River

Vance Lake

51

Lily pads on the lake DENICE BREAUX

Well-marked trails lead the way DENICE BREAUX

birch and aspen and little white pines. I'm a huge fan of bogs and relish any opportunity to walk through one and find myself stopping every 10 feet to look and listen.

About halfway around the loop, the trail meets the junction with the Lookout Trail, which also connects to the Little Bit Longer Loop (love that name), Statehouse Lake, and Big River Trails. Score great views of Statehouse Lake from here and then, still on the boardwalk trail, angle southeast and around the south end of the lake to the homestretch to the trailhead.

Why Go?

The NLDC is packed to the brim with conservation-focused events and activities. One of the most popular is the citizen science program, leveraging dedicated efforts from volunteer scientists to collect data for an array of research projects throughout Wisconsin. In addition to providing invaluable assistance to professional scientists, this program fosters enduring stewardship of our environment and introduces people, young and old alike, to new ways of engaging with nature.

Miles and Directions

0.0 Hike north from the trailhead on the Bog Boardwalk Trail.

0.1 Reach junction with the start of the boardwalk.

0.5 At the trail junction with outer trails, head southeast.

1.2 Arrive back at the trailhead.

15 Escanaba Lake Trail

It's tough to beat a color-coded trail system that escorts you through uber-scenic forest and past a collection of hidden lakes. This hike gets bonus points for a shelter and firepit situated along the way.

Distance: 4.5 miles, with options for additional miles
Difficulty: Moderate
Photogenic factor: 4
Hiking time: About 2 hours
Trail surface: Packed dirt and spongy pine needle duff
Other trail users: None
Canine compatibility: Leashed pets allowed

Land status: State forest
Fees and permits: Vehicle pass required
Maps: Escanaba Lake Ski Trail map; USGS White Sand Lake
Trail contacts: Northern Highland American Legion State Forest, 4125 CR M, Boulder Junction, WI 54512; (715) 356-9739; dnr. wisconsin.gov/topic/StateForests/nhal

Finding the trailhead: From Woodruff, follow US 51 north 6.4 miles to CR M. Turn right and head northeast 12.4 miles to Nebish Lake Road. Turn right and go 3.7 miles east to the trailhead parking entrance on the left. **Trailhead GPS:** N46 03.236' / W89 35.227'

The Hike

My cross-country skier friends all agree the Escanaba Lake Trail is one of the most scenic and exhilarating in the entire state. A bold statement, perhaps, and one my summertime view supports with verve. I was mesmerized every step of the way by wildflowers of red and white and orange, a weathered plank bridge, and teaser views through the trees of Pallette and Escanaba Lakes. All the while, the trail itself entertained with gentle undulations and little dips. The Northern Highland American Legion State Forest boasts more than 225,000 acres spread across Vilas, Oneida, and Iron Counties and includes three mighty rivers—the Wisconsin, Manitowish, and Flambeau. Visitors are treated to 900 lakes in the forest and nearly 250 bird species totaling 73 percent of the state's recorded species. Look and listen for scarlet tanager, whippoorwill, great horned owl, red-breasted nuthatch, pileated woodpecker, and ruby-throated hummingbirds. The forest is also home to one of the state's largest concentrations of nesting bald eagles. Common ground denizens include red fox, fisher, black bear, snowshoe hare, white-tailed deer, pine marten, and beaver. The forest is highlighted with birch, sugar maple, white and red pine, balsam fir, and assorted lower shrubbery. It all makes for a verdant green backdrop on this blissfully quiet lake loop.

Set off from the trailhead on the combination red, blue, yellow trail heading west and crunching tons of empty acorn shells under your boots. Start to finish, the path is virtually devoid of obstacles such as roots, intruding boulders, steep inclines, or stairs.

Tunnel of trees DENICE BREAUX

The only negative I saw was the hike's earliest section, strewn with old logs in messy piles like it was all tossed there by a storm. Other than that, expect quintessential Wisconsin North Country, and with these being ski trails, you'll have ample room to share conversation with a friend.

Hike west for just over 0.5 mile to a junction that sends the blue and yellow trails north. Stick to the red and green trails on a northwesterly course along a low-hanging ridge above the southern shore of Pallette Lake. The lake reveals itself through intermittent breaks in the trees until the trail passes the far northwestern bay. Curve around to the east and across the portage trail between Pallette and Lost Canoe Lakes. (Lost Canoe—what a great name for a lake.) For a convenient and short side trip, follow the portage trail to the right for a rest stop on Pallette's north side.

HIDDEN HEMLOCK TREASURE

Did you know that hemlock trees fueled a booming leather industry in the late 1800s? Tannins found in the bark of hemlocks were essential ingredients in the leather-tanning process. Millions of trees were felled and stripped of their bark, which was hauled to tanneries in cities such as Milwaukee. In the early 1900s, Wisconsin was the nation's leading supplier of "tanning bark." All the trees were gone, but at least you could have a wallet in your pocket.

Wooden bridge crossing (left); singletrack through the woods (right) DENICE BREAUX

Back on the main trail, continue trekking east-southeast to the trail shelter near the northwestern tip of Escanaba Lake. The blue and red trail keeps heading east from here for a nearly 8-mile loop, but today's route goes due south on the green trail, paralleling the western shore of Escanaba Lake, which sports an uncanny resemblance to a map of the US. A short dip in elevation from the trailhead is followed by a moderately long climb at about 5 percent, with scattered views of the lake at the top and a final downhill cruise to the trailhead.

Like other fortunate lakes in this area, Escanaba has been protected from permanent development under a state management plan ever since the establishment of Wisconsin's first forestry commission. You might also see a few trees near shore wrapped with flagging tape and round reflectors indicating specific study sites for periodic ecological research. In another boon, the lake was granted "wild lake" status in the 1980s to ensure continued protection from development.

Why Go?

Since 1946, the Northern Highland Fishery Research Area (formerly the Five Lakes Project) has studied fish catch limits on Escanaba, Nebish, Mystery, Spruce, and Pallette Lakes. The lakes are all located in the area between Boulder Junction and Star

Escanaba Lake Trail

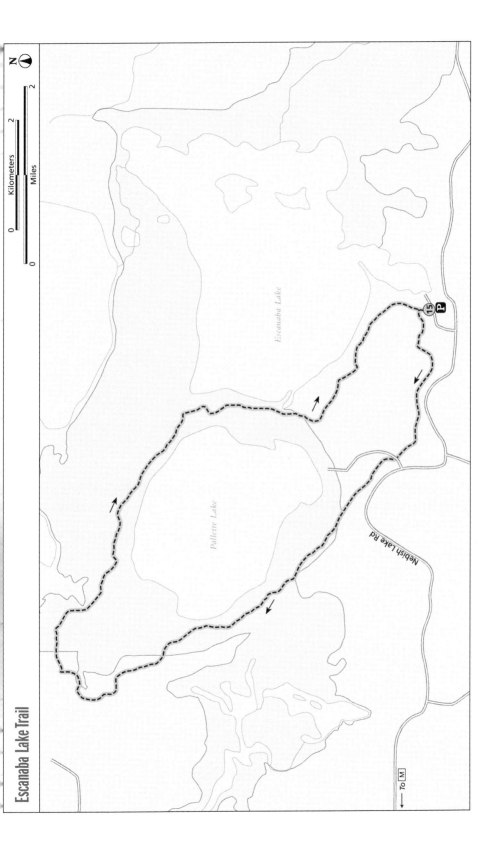

Home stretch to the trailhead DENICE BREAUX

Lake and the DNR-sponsored project is the longest running fisheries monitoring program in the country, with an integral connection between state conservation efforts, public access and use, and scientific research.

Miles and Directions

0.0   From the trailhead, hike westbound on the combination red, blue, yellow trail.

0.7   Reach junction where blue and yellow trails head north; stay on the red and green trail, bearing left (northwest).

2.6   Arrive at the junction with portage trail. Turn right if you want a quick break and then continue east/southeast on main trail.

3.2   Reach the trail shelter and junction; turn south following blue and green, then green and yellow trails.

4.5   Arrive back at the trailhead.

16 Plum Lake Hemlock Forest State Natural Area

This hike makes this author's picks for the best hikes in the state. A bold statement backed up by ridiculously beautiful scenery, heavenly trails, and conservation-based history.

Distance: 4.1 miles, with options for additional miles

Difficulty: Moderate

Photogenic factor: 5

Hiking time: About 2 hours

Trail surface: Hard-packed dirt

Other trail users: None

Canine compatibility: Pets not allowed on Star Lake Trail; leashed pets allowed in Plum Lake State Natural Area

Land status: State of Wisconsin

Fees and permits: None

Maps: DNR maps; USGS Wakefield, MI

Trail contacts: Wisconsin Department of Natural Resources, 101 S. Webster St., Madison, WI 53707; (888) 936-7463; dnr.wi.gov/topic/Lands/naturalareas/index.asp

Finding the trailhead: From the village of Star Lake at the junction of CR K and CR N, follow CR N south 0.9 mile to a skinny forest road just past the Star Lake East campground. Look for the little Trampers Trails sign. Follow that road 1 mile south to its end at the trailhead. **Trailhead GPS:** N46 01.293' / W89 47.185'

The Hike

This trail gets my vote for the best off-the-grid, way-out-there remote path. Tucked partly in the Plum Lake Hemlock Forest State Natural Area (SNA), this route is part of a wonderfully squiggly maze of a trail system that wanders the woods along the southern shore of Star Lake.

The path mixes it up with get-your-feet-wet close to the water, rugged sections of roots and rocks on punchy little hills and stretches of calm in the trees. This is yet another of my all-time favorite trails, in large part due to its remote vibe, old-growth forest lineage, and silent invitation to just go out there and do what it's named for: tramping!

With every step of this hike, know that you are traveling through a near-virgin stand of old-growth forest packed with the likes of relict hemlock, yellow and paper birch, sugar maple, and basswood. Forestry experts tell us that the presence of large, aged white birch means this stand likely was born of a fire event around 1810 with a natural succession of species from aspen to hemlock. Shrub species in attendance include mountain maple, honeysuckle, and elderberry; below you will see mayflower, plentiful emerald-green moss, snowberry, and lots more. Flitting about this paradise are dozens of songbird species, merrily singing the praises of calling this place home.

Hiking at water's edge DENICE BREAUX

We can join in their song, simultaneously content and proud to be in such good company and treasured legacy. SNAs like this one are Wisconsin's last refuges for rare plant and animal species. More than 90 percent of plants and 75 percent of endangered and threatened species in our state are protected within SNAs. Many of these places provide critical living laboratories for scientific research due to their visible evidence of natural processes evolving with very little human meddling. And that is the most priceless of heirlooms to share with generations to come.

The entire first half of the loop traces very close to Star Lake's shoreline with the expected gorgeous views. The trail is a blast, full of personality in the form of scattered boulders of various girth and of course the resplendent hemlock forest. At the top side of the western loop, the trail skirts around a little pond and it is here where, if you're ambitious, you can keep right on hiking for the rest of the day.

For this shorter option, however, head back south and link up with the connector trail along the shore back to the first loop and follow the southern leg of that loop back to the trailhead.

Plum Lake Hemlock Forest SNA

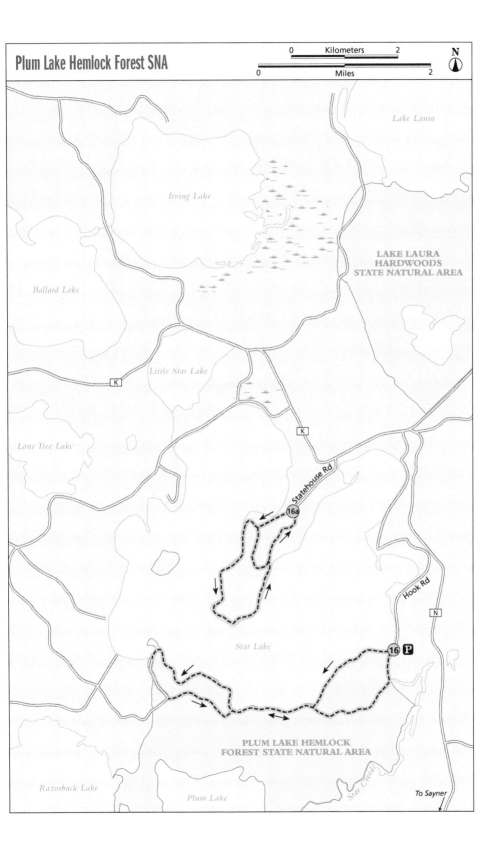

Star Lake view from the trail DENICE BREAUX

Why Go?

The Plum Lake Hemlock Forest State Natural Area was assigned as such in 1953 and boasts rare and humbling examples of big hemlocks, supported with accoutrements such as balsam fir, wood fern, white birch, tamarack, white pine, and many moss species. The red-eyed vireo nests here, as does the blackburnian warbler, northern parula, winter wren, and hermit thrush.

Miles and Directions

0.0 Follow the trail along the lake.

0.7 At the junction with the west side of the loop section of the trail, go straight ahead.

1.2 Take the right fork here, following the shoreline.

2.1 At the junction at the top side of this loop, head straight, going south.

2.4 Veer left at this junction.

2.8 Turn left here and make a quick right back along the shore trail.

3.3 At the junction with the first loop, go right and complete the circle back to the trailhead.

4.1 Arrive back at the trailhead. Don't miss the decadent Star Lake Trail just up the road (see details below):

16a Bonus Hike: Star Lake Trail

Distance: 2.5 miles
Difficulty: Easy to moderate
Photogenic factor: 4
Hiking time: About 90 minutes
Trail surface: Hard-packed dirt path
Other trail users: None
Canine compatibility: Pets not allowed on Star Lake Trail; leashed pets allowed in Plum Lake SNA

Land status: State of Wisconsin
Fees and permits: None
Maps: DNR maps; USGS Wakefield, MI
Trail contacts: Wisconsin Department of Natural Resources, 101 S. Webster St., Madison, WI 53707; (888) 936-7463; dnr.wi.gov/topic/Lands/naturalareas/index.asp

Finding the trailhead: From the town of Sayner, follow CR N 5.6 miles north to CR K and turn left. Follow CR K 0.5 mile west to Statehouse Road and turn left. In 0.4 mile this road ends at the trailhead. **Trailhead GPS:** N46 03.266' / W89 47.746'

The Hike

I'm just going to come right out and say it: These are my favorite hiking trails in the state. I relished every single step and more than one time had to pry myself away from one idyllic place only to be captivated by another. I'm no world traveler but I've been fortunate to hike all over the country, from oceanside getaways to the rarified air of mountaintops, and for all-around "unforgettableness," the short little Star Lake hike in northern Wisconsin is tops on the list.

Steeped in history and otherworldly scenery, this trail is made of ideal hiking tread, with a layer of pine needles and sandy soil creating a spongy feel that puts a natural spring in your step. Gnarled and determined roots furrow the trail, and boulders of various sizes punctuate the path in all the right places. Fittingly, the Star Lake Trail is located on a narrow peninsula jutting into its namesake lake, and to the joy of hikers everywhere, the trail traces the squiggly shoreline all the way around.

In some places the path takes you close enough to dip your toes in the lake (or jump right in). Other sections are elevated for stop-in-your-tracks views, especially on the eastern side, with beeline views of a pair of islands way across the lake. At the southern tip of the peninsula is a place that inspires all manner of nature-based daydreams: Elegant, soaring white pines shade a picnic-perfect scene, with a firepit and water's-edge views of the lake. There's even a little beach here for spontaneous swims. Heavenly.

From here the path shows off just enough up and down to make it interesting, and one of my favorite sights is a huge, shoreside cedar that tied itself into a knot as it grew around a boulder. A fascinating display of resolve, and I bet you can't untie that knot!

Shoreline trail DENICE BREAUX

This is a great path for all ages and abilities, made even better with its deep historical roots. Did you know that this peninsula hosted Wisconsin's first tree nursery, inspired by our first state forester? E. M. Griffith believed in replanting the Northland after the ravages of logging, and under his guidance, a red pine plantation plot was planted here in 1913 with seedlings grown at the old Trout Lake Nursery in Boulder Junction. Griffith planted native red and white pine, along with Scotch pine for its rapid growth rate. Today you can see vivid evidence of the plantation experiment and walk among the giant trees.

Hike west from the trailhead, down a gradual slope to a quick left, following the nature trail sign. Keep heading southwest (right) and cross a scenic boardwalk section, then emerge to 180-degree views of the lake. From here the path traces the shoreline on a super-fun, gently undulating track to the southern end of the peninsula. Here is where you'll find that cover-shot picnic spot and you can't go any farther without stopping to savor this place—those are the rules.

Roll on from here up along the western shore, with more exquisite views that will make you stumble over your own feet. After the trail turns inland, it meets one more junction where you'll turn left and wander through another stand of regal pines on the way back to the trailhead.

As a close to this chapter, I'd like you to think about the 1800s logging mania. In a sixteen-year blink of time, original centuries-old forest was razed. The people came, took what they wanted, and left behind nothing but stumps and rubble. Today, far more people are of the same mindset, and for lack of better words, we are beating our planet into submission. I hope more of us will channel our inner E. M. Griffith or Leopold or Muir and work to save more special places like this.

Miles and Directions

0.0 From the trailhead, hike due west on the main path.
0.2 Turn left here toward the lake.
1.6 Take the right fork here and pass through a bog area.
2.1 Take a left turn back to the trailhead.
2.5 Arrive back at the trailhead.

THERE AND GONE

Following a very familiar refrain in the logging era, the bustling town of Star Lake emerged virtually overnight in the late 1800s, with around 600 hardy souls hustling about a menagerie of warehouses, offices, a hotel, a school, and a railroad depot. And it was all about trees. An estimated 2 billion board feet of pine timber was logged clear from lands around Star Lake. When the trees were gone, the town disappeared as well.

17 Drummond Loop

One of the area's most popular cross-country ski trail clusters makes a splendid warm-weather hiking destination. Don't miss it in fall's fiery colors.

Distance: 3.5 miles, with options for additional miles
Difficulty: Easy to moderate
Photogenic factor: 4
Hiking time: 1 hour
Trail surface: Hard-packed dirt and grass
Other trail users: An occasional mountain bike
Canine compatibility: Leashed pets allowed

Land status: Chequamegon National Forest
Fees and permits: Vehicle pass required
Maps: National forest maps; USGS Diamond Lake
Trail contacts: Chequamegon National Forest, 500 Hanson Lake Rd., Rhinelander, WI 54501; (715) 362-1300; fs.usda.gov/cnnf

Finding the trailhead: From US 63 in Drummond, follow North Lake Owen Drive 0.9 mile to the trailhead parking area on the left. **Trailhead GPS:** N46 32.449' / W91 24.095'

The Hike

Attracted by immense stands of white and Norway pine in the late 1800s, the Rust-Owen Lumber Company eyed northern Wisconsin as a fine place to build a sawmill. At the time, The Chicago, St. Paul, Minneapolis, and Omaha Railway was laying a line inexorably north to Lake Superior. Crew leader Frank Drummond supervised construction of the mill, shack houses, barns, and a company store, all owned by the lumber company. Rust-Owen later established their own railroad, the Drummond & South Western, to help ship lumber to various markets. The "town" was soon named after Frank Drummond.

Today, only relic stands of Wisconsin's once grand and noble forests remain. One of them is adjacent to this chapter's hike and ski trails and I highly recommend a visit. Drummond Woods (and associated Scientific and Natural Area) hosts old-growth northern mesic hardwoods, including 40-inch hemlocks, soaring red and white pine, sugar maple, birch, ash, and basswood, all scattered over rolling terrain and hummocks of forest detritus. A 0.75-mile interpretive trail lopes through the site's understory of various tree species saplings, honeysuckle, hazelnut, ferns, moss, and grasses. Swales and scattered transient ponds are home to flora such as mountain wood sorrel and lilies.

Across Highway 63 and a short walk along the North Country Trail, hikers will find an additional 23 miles of trails maintained by the Drummond Area Ski Trails Association. Arranged in a cluster of loops from about 1.5 to 6 miles, the trails wind through handsome forest of mixed hardwood, spruce, and white pine sprouting from gently undulating topography. In winter, the classic skiing-only trails are a favorite for new skiers, family outings, and intermediate skiers honing their skills. In

Peaceful, fern-lined trail

Classic Northwoods Wisconsin

warm-weather months, this a great place for a hike. I'm generally not a fan of hiking on cross-country ski trails, as they typically feel like wide, grass-covered roadways, but these paths are more intimate and there's a fun bonus hike to the Lake Owen picnic area and beach for a refreshing swim on steamy summer days. Best of all, the North Country Trail bisects the Drummond trails, making this an ideal launch pad for extended wilderness junkets.

From the trailhead, hike east on the Boulevard Trail and take the first left. This is the return stretch of the Jackrabbit Trail and follows a series of barely-there elevation changes to a long-lazy curve northeast. You'll pass a few giant white pines tucked among this stunning Northwoods forest as the path continues its oval-shaped course back south to a junction with the Boulevard's southbound option to Lake Owen. Pass the Racetrack, Antler, and Jackrabbit junctions on the homestretch back to the trailhead.

If you don't make the side trip to Lake Owen on the trail, be sure to visit another time. This compact, tidy picnic area hosts a small shelter with stone fireplace overlooking an idyllic setting of stately pines and sand beach. Beyond is one of Wisconsin's clearest and most scenic lakes and that's a bold statement—clear, scenic lakes are everywhere up here. Part of the Chequamegon-Nicolet National Forest, Lake Owen stretches roughly 7 miles between Cable and Drummond and is steeped in regional lore. Sioux and Chippewa people lived in and explored this region for generations, followed by European settlers and the fur trade. Logging transformed the entire area in the mid-1800s, and a rail line from Spooner in 1880 inspired the rough and tumble

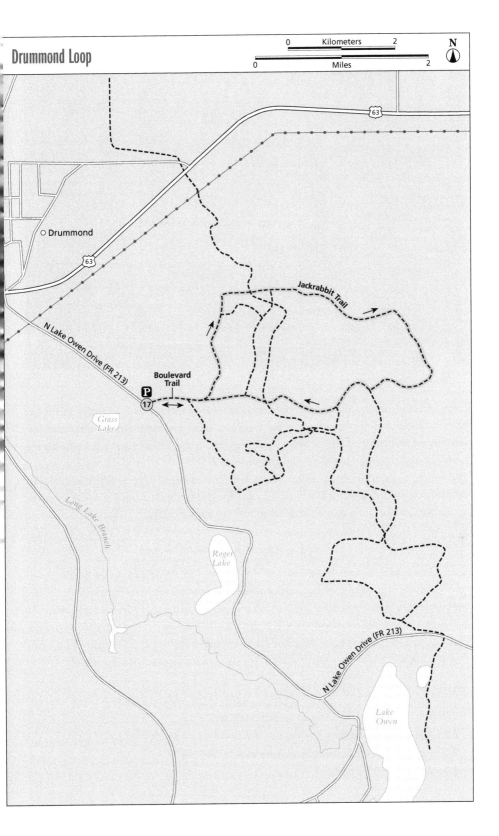

North Country Trail crossing

town of Cable, made of rowdy saloons, general stores, and hotels. Lumberjacks mixed with railroad and construction crews until an 1882 fire destroyed the ramshackle settlement and most of the people packed up and left. But less than a decade later, a new population migrated here and resurrected Cable as a tourist destination. Peace and quiet, and hundreds of clean, clear lakes, also attracted "city folks" interested in building cabins for weekend getaways. Lake Owen quickly became a popular location for resorts and posh homes and the tradition continues today.

Why Go?

Lake Owen Hardwoods State Natural Area is a mile-wide peninsula hosting one of Wisconsin's most native and undisturbed forests. Old-growth hemlocks grow in unfragmented stands near the lake's shoreline, along with paper birch, maple, red oak, and aspen. Scattered among Pennsylvania sedge below are Canada mayflower, aster, club moss, and other species. Seepage lakes include bog/muskeg environments with floating aquatic plants and fern swamps. Moose are occasional visitors as well.

Miles and Directions

0.0 From the tailhead, hike east on the Boulevard Trail.
0.2 Turn left on Jackrabbit.
2.3 Pass junction with Boulevard's southern track to Lake Owen.
3.5 Arrive back at the trailhead.

18 Hunt Hill Audubon Sanctuary

Farsighted conservation vision appears again in northern Wisconsin at this 600-acre vestige of restored native prairie, forests, and lakes, and Wilderness Society lineage.

Distance: 2.8 miles, with options for additional miles
Difficulty: Easy with one moderate climb
Photogenic factor: 5
Hiking time: 1 hour
Trail surface: Hard-packed dirt
Other trail users: None

Canine compatibility: Leashed pets allowed
Land status: Hunt Hill Audubon Sanctuary
Fees and permits: None
Maps: Sanctuary maps; USGS Nobleton
Trail contacts: Hunt Hill Audubon Sanctuary, N2384 Hunt Hill Rd., Sarona, WI 54870; (715) 635-6543; hunthill.org

Finding the trailhead: From Sarona at CR D and US 53, follow CR D 1 mile to CR P and turn left. In 0.5 mile, turn right on Audubon Road and head east 2.4 miles to Hunt Hill Road. Turn left; the sanctuary entrance is 0.2 mile on the right. **Trailhead GPS:** N45 72.083' / W91 73.563'

The Hike

Imagine a refuge protecting some of Wisconsin's most celebrated habitats. Imagine a place that protects rare bogs, diverse forests with remnant old-growth, open meadows, and clear glacial lakes. Throw in early 1900s wilderness spirit and you have a generations-proud homestead-turned-haven built on nature education and the work of some of America's most celebrated conservationists.

Hunt Hill began with a very traditional story. When someone in Wisconsin or Minnesota asks "Whacha doin' this weekend?" a common refrain is, "Oh, we're heading up north to the cabin." Seems every other family in the neighborhood has a place on a lake somewhere north of their day-to-day abode and during our short summers around here, we go "up north." Mine is one of those families and I treasure every cabin-y moment, just like the Andrews household. Drawn to northern Wisconsin's lakes and woods in the early 1900s, Arthur Andrews leveraged his successful post as a Minneapolis grain merchant to acquire a cabin in a chunk of woods east of Sarona. The little cabin sat on a hill above a pair of lakes and the Andrews named it Hunt Hill in honor of Mrs. Andrews's family. When a for-sale sign went up at an adjoining farm, Arthur scooped up the property, along with additional land in northern Minnesota and Michigan, to expand their wilderness retreats.

The Andrews clan lived with a strong conservation mindset, pervasive at the time with much of the country, and their wilderness ideals developed into working relationships with environmental luminaries, including Aldo Leopold, Ernest Oberholtzer, Roger Tory Peterson, and others who influenced the formation of the

The Bear Trail blaze (left); the bog boardwalk (right)

Wilderness Society. In fact, Leopold launched forestry studies at Hunt Hill in the early 1930s, efforts that continue today in Wisconsin's longest running forest research.

To our heartfelt gratitude, Arthur's daughter Frances donated the Andrews estate to the National Audubon Society to be used for nature education in a classroom that includes 600 acres with 13 miles of hiking trails, the family's two original cabins, recreation hall, library, dorms, and a stacked calendar of outdoors-based activities. The Bear Trail is a great way to experience what Hunt Hill is all about, on a squiggly loop circling Upper and Lower Twin Lakes from the main camp.

From the main parking area, stroll east past the impeccably restored farmstead outbuildings and barn to the start of the Barred Owl Trail, skirting the edge of the sanctuary's expansive prairie. A short spur trail to the bog boardwalk is a must-do for an intimate encounter with a rare vestige of a northern bog environment, filled with aromas of tamarack, vibrant sphagnum moss, and assorted diminutive flora like the insect-trapping pitcher plant and sundew. Orchids color the bog in June and July. I'm a huge fan of bogs and this one's a classic. Did you know that thick mats of peat like this are like cryogenic preservers? In some places of the world, peat bogs have hosted human remains dating back thousands of years!

From the boardwalk, the trail lopes back uphill and traces the woods-prairie boundary around Heron Point to a Wisconsin Conservation Corps (WCC) foot-bridge over a channel flowing into Lower Twin Lake. Past the bridge, the trail winds through resplendent northern hardwood forest over gentle undulations to a balcony bluff view of Big Devil's Lake. A wooden bench offers a splendid opportunity to relax with the gorgeous Northwoods scene. Look aloft for osprey sightings; an active

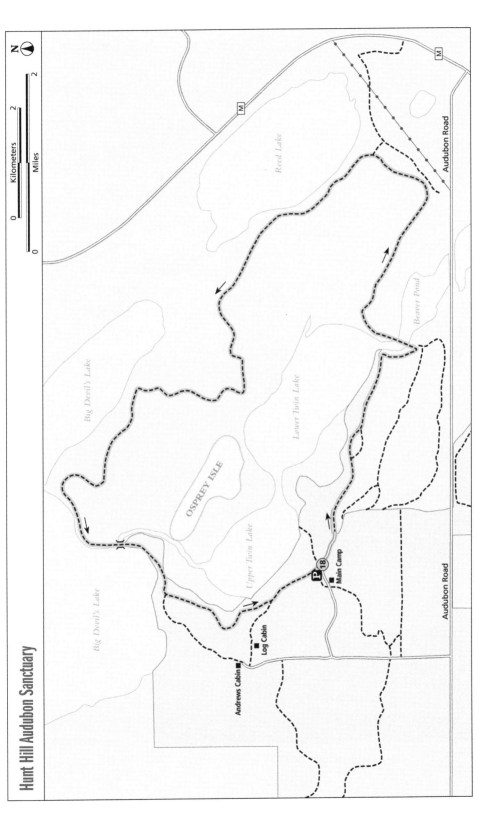

Hunt Hill Audubon Sanctuary

Trailside view of Big Devil's Lake

Lake view from a footbridge

nesting platform sits just to the southeast of another short footbridge. Cross the bridge and, from here, the trail leads back into dense forest and a long, moderately steep grade back to the main camp and trailhead.

Why Go?

As habitat loss continues unabated, native sphagnum bogs are increasingly rare. Hunt Hill has two, one of which is a designated State Natural Area. Dory's Bog, 2 miles from the site's main camp, includes a small bog lake surrounded by successional ecological zones. The bog is loaded with diverse flora including cranberries, pitcher plant, bog laurel, sedge, and orchids. Favorable habitat and food sources attract a robust songbird population. Sounds and sights of crested flycatcher, red-eyed vireo, rose-breasted grosbeak, hermit thrush, and a host of others are common at the bog and throughout the sanctuary.

Miles and Directions

0.0 Hike east from the trailhead, past the barn and other main camp buildings.

0.1 At the junction with the prairie trail, follow the Barred Owl Trail into the woods.

0.2 Turn left on the bog boardwalk.

0.5 Cross the WCC footbridge.

2.2 Reach and enjoy Big Devil's Lake viewpoint, then cross another bridge.

2.8 Arrive back at the trailhead.

19 Nugget Lake Trails

A UFO vibe accompanies off-the-grid solitude at this compact, densely wooded park. Its namesake lake offers excellent fishing and paddling options.

Distance: 3 miles, with options for additional miles
Difficulty: Easy
Photogenic factor: 4
Hiking time: 75 minutes
Trail surface: Hard-packed dirt
Other trail users: None

Canine compatibility: Leashed pets allowed
Land status: County park
Fees and permits: Vehicle pass required
Maps: Park maps; USGS Plum City
Trail contacts: Nugget Lake County Park, N4351 County Rd HH, Plum City, WI 54761

Finding the trailhead: From WI 29 and CR CC in Spring Valley, follow CC south 9.2 miles to CR HH and turn left. Follow HH 2.1 miles to the park entrance. The hike starts at the bottom of the hill. **Trailhead GPS:** N44 69.232' / W92 22.447'

The Hike

Welcome to UFO country. Wisconsin's version of Area 51. As far back as the mid-1970s, the lands between Elmwood and Maiden Rock have been UFO attractors. In fact, Elmwood's self-proclaimed tagline is UFO Capital of Wisconsin, and the little town proudly hosts an annual UFO Days celebration.

Arguably the most famous extraterrestrial tale is of the night in 1975 when Elmwood's chief of police investigated a bright light on the other side of a hill. Plane crash? House fire? When he arrived at the site, however, he said he saw a football field–sized saucer hovering above the trees. The chief spotted another saucer a year later, but this time the mysterious ship fired some kind of ray gun at his squad car. In a different incident, a flying saucer allegedly landed on a deserted county road, right in front of a surprised and terrified local mother and her children. A local farmer followed them home, but the UFO did too. It's unclear what happened next.

What gives? Do aliens like cheese or the Green Bay Packers? And it's not only UFOs; a giant meteorite targeted this area as well, landing smack dab in today's Nugget Lake County Park. The resulting 4-mile-wide crater created the Blue Rock formation, a stack of limestone tilted at angles from its original resting place.

This fun hike skirts the boundary of the former crater, and a pair of spur trails lead to an overlook with a splendid vista and an underlook for a unique geologic vantage point.

Made of roughly 750 acres of rolling woods, Nugget Lake County Park is named for the lake of the same name that spawns Plum Creek, which flows slowly southeast to its confluence with the Chippewa River. Blissfully off the beaten path, this place is rarely crowded, and the trail system feels like a private backyard wilderness. Arranged

The trail in a meadow to forest transition

in a stacked series of clusters from 0.2 mile to 1.5 miles, the color-coded trails take hikers over hill and dale blanketed in thick hardwood forest, and along riparian corridors of Pine, Rock Elm, and Plum Creeks, with a handful of bridge crossings en route. This short day hike follows the western and topside perimeter of the park and then delves toward the center to take in the underlook and overlook at Blue Rock.

From the trailhead, follow the orange trail north, turning left (northwest) at all junctions. The paths here are two-hikers wide and grassy, mowed short, so walking is easy, but know this: Mosquitoes love it here and will descend upon you as if you were in some kind of creepy horror movie. Even covered in DEET one late summer day, we ran/hiked just to stay clear of the buggers. Best advice? Shoot for a cool fall day after a frost.

Roughly the first mile of the hike trends uphill, on the orange and brown trails, to a bridge crossing over Pine Creek on a stubby section of the red trail. Turn left again on the green trail and follow a lazy crescent northbound on the black trail, cross a bridge over Rock Elm Creek, and a right turn on the yellow trail. After about 0.3 mile, the path hairpins and meets the blue trail, which parallels the creek back to the black trail and onward to a spur trail to the Blue Rock underlook, named for the close-up view of the underbelly of this ancient rock upheaval of 480-million-year-old dolostone. Geologists tell us the aforementioned meteor created a crater that was 0.75 mile deep and 4 miles across. Named the Rock Elm Disturbance, this evidence of violent earthen strife generated supersonic shock waves and an explosion akin to a hydrogen bomb. The enormous crater has long since filled in, of course, after 470 million years of fascinating geologic phenomena.

Bulbous nose of Blue Rock at creekside

Nugget Lake Trails

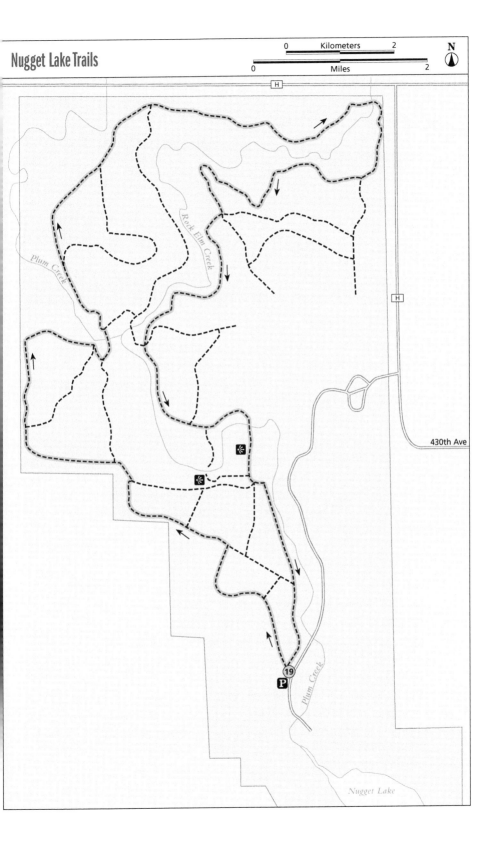

Kilometers
0   2

Miles
0   2

N

H

Rock Elm Creek

Plum Creek

H

430th Ave

19
P

Plum Creek

Nugget Lake

Trail to the underlooks

After the underlooks, backtrack to the black trail and hike south across the creek to another spur trail to the overlook, with fine views of the narrow creek valley from the top of the Blue Rock formation. Retrace your tracks to the black trail and follow it southbound to the trailhead.

Why Go?

The Nugget Lake area makes geologists swoon. Right around 470 million years ago, a meteorite roughly 550 feet in diameter blasted to the ground here at 60,000 miles per hour, with the force of a hydrogen bomb, causing an unfathomable explosion that heaved huge layers of dolomite limestone at steep angles. The so-called Rock Elm Disturbance created what we see today, known as Blue Rock.

Miles and Directions

0.0 Follow the orange trail north from the trailhead, always hiking to the left (northwest).

0.5 Turn left on the brown trail, following its perimeter to the red trail.

0.9 Buttonhook on the red trail to the green trail and turn left.

1.4 Reach the junction with the black trail; continue straight/left (east).

1.8 Cross Rock Elm Creek and reach the junction with the yellow trail; turn right.

2.3 Reach the junction with the blue trail; turn right.

2.4 Reach the junction with the black trail; turn left.

2.6 Reach the spur trail to the underlook. After the view, backtrack to the black trail.

2.7 Reach the side trail to the overlook. After the view, backtrack to the black trail and follow it south to the trailhead.

3.0 Arrive back at the trailhead.

Door County and Lake Michigan Shoreline

The Great Mitten Debate carries on in good fun up here in the Northland. For generations, Wisconsin's shape has been likened to mittens or plump potholders, with giant thumbs making waves in Green Bay and Lake Michigan. The "thumb" is formally known as the Door County Peninsula, renowned all o'er the land for its 300 miles of spectacularly beautiful shoreline, five state parks, delectable fruit orchards, diverse wildlife habitat, and lively community festivals. But Michigan's Lower Peninsula also looks like a mitten, so which state gets the mitten moniker? We all need two mittens to get through winter up here, right? And Michigan's Keweenaw Peninsula looks like the beanie of a goofy winter hat, so we're ready for snow!

Regardless of resemblance to cold-weather attire, Door County is a special place. Locals already know as much, and more than 2 million visitors traveling here every year enthusiastically agree. The Door has eleven historic lighthouses. It has fresh cherry pie and refreshing local brews. It's loaded with parks and seductive waters for sailboats, paddleboats, kayaks, or just for jumping in! And I can't get enough of the little towns on both shores, bursting with character and a unique "Door" vibe. I have favorites shore to shore, including Egg Harbor, named one of America's best small towns with a classic main street and wildly talented artisans. Ephraim has Wilson's Ice Cream Parlor ('nuff said). Newport State Park is an International Dark Sky Reserve. Washington and Rock Islands are life list camping getaways. Gills Rock is steeped in maritime history with a Norman Rockwell village flanked by high bluffs, and I love Baileys Harbor for its nature preserves and peaceful beaches.

Whatever your pleasure, Door County has it, and you're bound to find new adventures too. Looking for more? Trickle down the shoreline to the south to must-hike lakeside parks such as Point Beach and Kohler-Andrae. And don't miss Milwaukee's outdoors vibe on the Lakefront Trail or Seven Bridges Trail.

20 Newport State Park

Plan some after-dark time at Wisconsin's only designated wilderness park. Named a Dark Sky Preserve in 2017 by the International Dark Sky Association, Newport is a stargazing delight; the perfect complement to 30 miles of some of the state's best hiking trails. This pair of loop trails shows off the park's different personalities.

Distance: 3.5 miles, with options for additional miles
Difficulty: Easy to moderate
Photogenic factor: 5
Hiking time: About 90 minutes
Trail surface: Sand and cordwalk
Other trail users: None
Canine compatibility: Leashed pets allowed

Land status: State park
Fees and permits: Vehicle pass required
Maps: Park maps; USGS Spider Island and Marinette
Trail contacts: Newport State Park, 475 CR NP, Ellison Bay, WI 54210; (920) 854-2500; dnr.wi.gov/topic/parks/name/newport

Finding the trailhead: From Ellison Bay, follow WI 42 2.3 miles east to CR NP and turn right. Go south and east on CR NP 2.5 miles to Newport Lane and turn right (south) again. Follow this road 0.8 mile to the park entrance and head to the end of the park road to the trailhead. **Trailhead GPS:** N45 23.455' / W86 99.767'

The Hike

With more and more people every single day on this orb we call home, we are sadly and very rapidly losing quiet places. Places without streetlights and yard lights, without a dog barking or the drone of traffic. Places where we can look up to a sky filled with endless constellations of jewels.

The good people at the International Dark Sky Association are working to save some quiet for us today and for our children tomorrow by preserving "land possessing exceptional or distinguished quality of starry nights and a protected nocturnal environment." This visionary nonprofit has designated select sites around the world as International Dark Sky Parks, and Newport is Wisconsin's first.

Newport's designation as a wilderness park (Wisconsin's only one) makes it even better, with few paved roads or light sources and an ideal location along Lake Michigan and the northern tip of the Door Peninsula. That's music to my ears, especially with 30 miles of trails squiggling around meadows, boreal forest, and 11 miles of rugged shoreline. You can see dark skies and a star or three from anywhere in the park, but three specific locations offer especially good viewing. Check park maps for the scoop.

In addition to dark skies, Newport State Park has sixteen primo hike-in campsites, a swimming beach, naturalist programs, and snowshoeing and cross-country skiing in winter.

Easygoing trail through the woods

It wasn't always this rosy. When interest in the land on this part of the Door increased, the State of Wisconsin envisioned a big-revenue facility like Peninsula State Park with heavy day use and a huge campground. The locals were vociferously opposed, fought the proposal, and won. That victory led to our first wilderness state park, which keeps the area in its most natural state. Development is not allowed, so our children and theirs will see this wonderful place just as it is today.

Newport State Park's hiking trails are the way to experience it best, and away we go. From the trailhead, the Newport Trail hugs the shoreline along Sand Cove. Phenomenal views appear from openings in the forest as the trail curves around a stub of land on the way to Duck Bay. Farther south, back on the Newport Trail, a trio of to-die-for campsites are situated along the shore and there's another deeper in the woods. I highly recommend spending a night or two out here.

A short track west leads to the topside of the Newport Trail and the option to check out views from Varney Point and extend the loop south and north along part of Rowleys Bay. Today, however, turn back northeast here and hike through the quiet conifer-hardwood forest toward the Sand Cove junction and the homestretch back to the trailhead.

Lagoon and Trifid Doug Earnest

Why Go?

Fly over the US at night and you'll see it lit up like a starry sky. And that's the problem—the map is backwards. The twinkling is supposed to come from above, but much of the population can't see it for the light pollution running rampant from coast to coast. With virtually no effort from officials to address the glaring issue, groups like the International Dark Sky Association are worth their weight in nebulas. We need places like Newport State Park or a New Mexico desert plateau or the middle of Lake Superior; places beyond imitation light that let us see and, if even for a moment, appreciate the peace of darkness.

Miles and Directions

0.0 Hike south from the trailhead, branching left along the shore where the Newport Trail continues south. Follow the Sand Cove-Duck Bay Trail.

1.4 Reach junction with the Newport Trail and turn left, passing some of the lakeside campsites.

2.1 Reach junction with Ridge Trail; turn right and follow the Ridge and Newport Trails back to the trailhead. (A left turn here [south] leads to Varney Point.)

3.5 Arrive back at the trailhead.

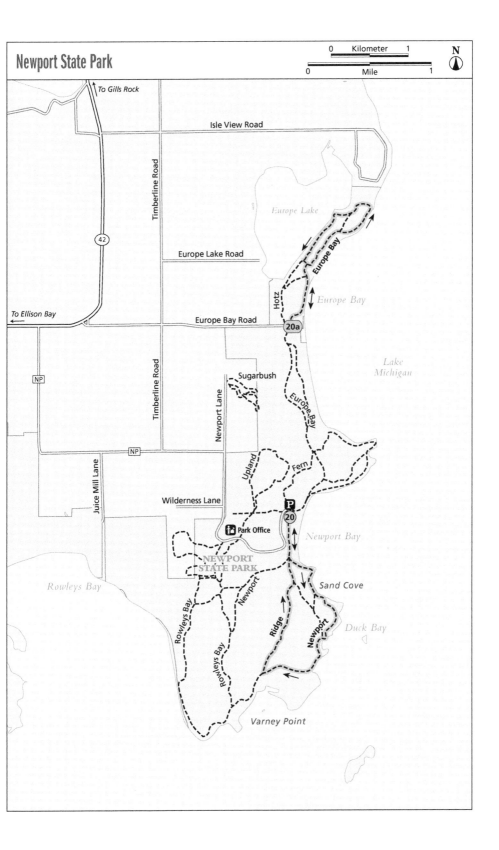

Newport State Park

0 Kilometer 1

0 Mile 1

N

To Gills Rock

Isle View Road

Timberline Road

42

Europe Lake

Europe Lake Road

Europe Bay

To Ellison Bay

Europe Bay Road

Hotz

Europe Bay

20a

Lake Michigan

NP

Sugarbush

Timberline Road

Newport Lane

Europe Bay

NP

Upland

Fern

Juice Mill Lane

Wilderness Lane

P

20

Park Office

Newport Bay

NEWPORT STATE PARK

Rowleys Bay

Sand Cove

Newport

Rowleys Bay

Ridge

Newport

Duck Bay

Rowleys Bay

Varney Point

20a Bonus Hike: Europe Lake Loop

Distance: 3-mile lollipop loop
Difficulty: Easy to moderate
Photogenic factor: 5

Hiking time: About 75 minutes
Trail surface: Sand, packed dirt, and cordwalk

Finding the trailhead: From the park office, head north on Newport Lane to CR NP and go west 0.5 mile to Timberline Road. Turn right and head north again 1 mile to Europe Bay Road. Turn right and find the trailhead in 1.1 miles at Liberty Grove Town Park. The trail starts at the road and goes north. **Trailhead GPS:** N45 25.942' / W86 98.600'

The Hike

Starting from Liberty Grove Town Park, this short loop follows the thin strip of land between Lake Michigan and Europe Lake, passing along sand dunes and seagrass on its earliest sections and then into the woods. Other than slight undulations in terra firma, the trail remains largely flat. (Expect somewhat hillier sections on the Hotz Trail at the northern end of the loop.)

At the trail's northern end, you'll loop to the eastern shore of camel-shaped Europe Lake and finish the loop southbound back to Europe Bay Road and the trailhead. Want more miles? Get seven of them by starting from the main park area or adding the loop south of the Liberty Grove Town Park trailhead.

Insider's tip: Europe Lake's maximum depth is only 10 feet. That means it warms up quickly and is great for swimming or floating a canoe.

Miles and Directions

0.0 Hike north on the Europe Bay Trail in the woods, paralleling the shoreline.
1.0 Reach the junction with the Hotz Trail, turn right. Hug the shore and then reconnect with the Europe Bay Trail. Follow Europe Bay north to the Hotz Trail.
1.6 Turn right at Hotz, round the peninsula, and hike south, close to the eastern shore of Europe Lake
2.3 Reach junction with the Europe Bay Trail and turn right to return to the trailhead.
3.0 Arrive back at the trailhead.

THE DARK OF NIGHT

Founded in 1988, the International Dark-Sky Association (IDA) is the world's oldest organization dedicated to preserving our dark sky heritage. IDA has made an enormous impact, helping make places like Newport State Park possible and continuing to lead the way away from the light. Visit their info-packed website at darksky.org.

21 Nicolet Loop–Peninsula State Park

Get a twofer at this spectacularly beautiful park on the Green Bay side of the Door Peninsula. A pair of loop trails serves up stop-in-your-tracks views, rugged and easy-going hiking, and an 1860s lighthouse.

Distance: 3.8 miles, with many options for additional miles
Difficulty: Mix of easy to challenging
Photogenic factor: 5+
Hiking time: 90 minutes to 2 hours
Trail surface: Hard-packed dirt
Other trail users: None

Canine compatibility: Leashed pets allowed
Land status: State park
Fees and permits: Vehicle pass required
Maps: Park maps; USGS Ephraim
Trail contacts: Peninsula State Park, 9462 Shore Rd., Fish Creek, WI 54212; (920) 868-3258; dnr.wi.gov/topic/parks/name/peninsula

Finding the trailhead: From Sturgeon Bay, follow WI 42 north for 22 miles to the village of Fish Creek. The main park entrance is just east of town but continue on WI 42 for 3 miles to the eastern entry at Shore Road. Turn left and follow Shore Road 1 mile north and take the Eagle Terrace fork to the right. The parking area and trailhead are 0.1 mile farther on the left. **Trailhead GPS:** N45 16.081' / W87 19.532'

The Hike

The first hunter-gatherer clans who lived in this area 11,000 years ago knew a good thing when they saw it. Today's Peninsula State Park is otherworldly gorgeous and chock full of amazing sights. How does 8 miles of shoreline; high, rocky bluffs; a vertical cedar forest; and a who's who of wildlife species sound? Did I mention Peninsula boasts two of Wisconsin's State Natural Areas? The White Cedar Forest and Beech Maple Forest State Natural Areas are loaded with all manner of flora and fauna providing critical habitats and research environments. Throw in sandy beaches and wildly popular summer theater performances and Peninsula checks all the boxes.

This is Wisconsin's second state park, established in 1909, and after a slow but gradual start, a go-to destination for the outdoor-minded. Door County Days, a summer festival with picnics, music, and sports, attracted thousands and the park soon transformed into one of the Midwest's premier active-interest locations. Today it is known as Wisconsin's most complete, albeit crowded, park, boasting nearly 500 campsites, group camps, outdoor theater, golf course, beach, miles of trails, and a lighthouse. Plenty for everyone, that's for sure.

Feel like taking it easy? Stroll along the Sunset Trail near Eagle Bluff Lighthouse for views of Green Bay and a cluster of islands to the west. For a more rugged day out, head east to the Sentinel and Eagle Trails. Whatever your pleasure, you'll find it here.

Nicolet Bay and Horseshoe Island DENICE BREAUX

And you won't be alone. Peninsula's list of critters includes seldom-seen crustaceans, globally rare snails, and unique ferns living in microhabitats in the park's cliffs. Larger and more mobile species are plentiful here as well, such as white-tailed deer, foxes, porcupines, grouse, turkey, and rabbits. In the trees and overhead are roughly 125 species of birds such as warblers, orioles, bluebirds, cardinals, and various raptors.

This is indeed a very active place and not just above ground. The cliffs at Peninsula are part of the expansive Niagara Escarpment, a limestone ridge stretching across nearly all of Wisconsin, part of Ontario, Canada, and on to the netherworld beneath Niagara Falls. Impressive, especially considering the escarpment started out as plain ol' mud at the bottom of an enormous saltwater sea that covered this area. The ridge took shape about 430 million years ago and today provides the launch pad for the mighty Niagara Falls.

This hike sets off from the Eagle Terrace parking area and does a little duckbill loop before tracing the ridge along the shoreline of Nicolet Bay. Enjoy breathtaking views of the bay and Horseshoe Island as the path drops down close to the shore to the Minnehaha Trail, then makes a steady climb south with one steep section back up to the top of the ridge. The Lone Pine Trail takes you through resplendent northern mesic forest of maple, beech, aspen, and scattered conifers, connecting with the Sentinel Trail.

Follow Sentinel on an easy climb back across Highland Road to return to the trailhead. Note that a couple sections of this loop travel over mildly challenging (fun) terrain of rocks and roots.

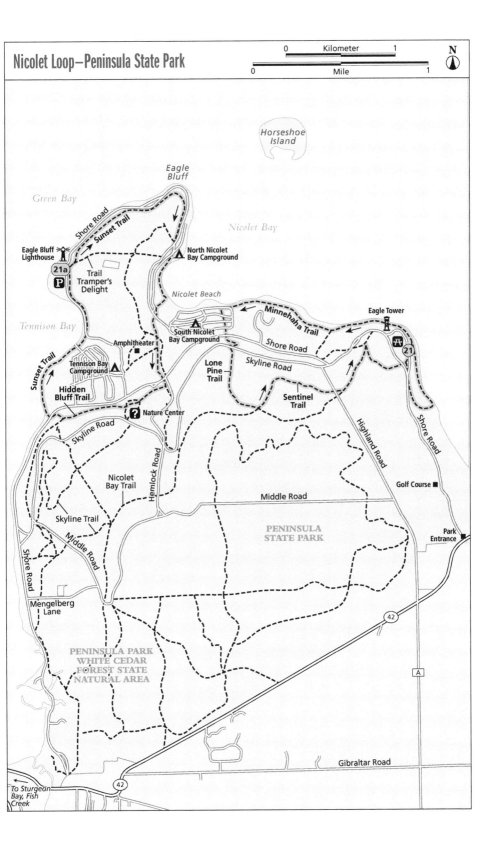

Nicolet Loop–Peninsula State Park

Horseshoe Island

Eagle Bluff

Green Bay

Shore Road

Sunset Trail

Nicolet Bay

Eagle Bluff Lighthouse

21a

P

Trail Tramper's Delight

North Nicolet Bay Campground

Nicolet Beach

Minnehaha Trail

Eagle Tower

21

Tennison Bay

Sunset Trail

South Nicolet Bay Campground

Amphitheater

Tennison Bay Campground

Shore Road

Skyline Road

Lone Pine Trail

Hidden Bluff Trail

Nature Center

Sentinel Trail

Shore Road

Skyline Road

Highland Road

Golf Course

Nicolet Bay Trail

Hemlock Road

Middle Road

PENINSULA STATE PARK

Skyline Trail

Park Entrance

Middle Road

Shore Road

Mengelberg Lane

42

PENINSULA PARK WHITE CEDAR FOREST STATE NATURAL AREA

A

Gibraltar Road

42

To Sturgeon Bay, Fish Creek

0   Kilometer   1

0   Mile   1

N

Splendid view of Nicolet Bay DENICE BREAUX

Miles and Directions

0.0 From the trailhead, follow the Eagle Trail signs and hike briefly southeast, looping back north along the shore of Nicolet Bay.

1.0 Reach the junction with the Minnehaha Trail, turn right.

1.6 Reach the junction with Lone Pine Trail, turn left.

2.4 Reach the junction with Sentinel Trail, turn left, crossing Highland Road shortly after.

3.3 Reach the junction with Eagle Trail, turn right.

3.8 Arrive back at the trailhead.

21a Bonus Hike: Sunset Loop

Distance: 3.8-mile loop, with many options for additional miles
Difficulty: Moderate

Photogenic factor: 5+
Hiking time: 90 minutes to 2 hours
Trail surface: Hard-packed dirt and paved

Finding the trailhead: From Sturgeon Bay, follow WI 42 north for 22 miles to the village of Fish Creek. The main park entrance is just east of town at Shore Road. Turn left and follow Shore Road 3.1 miles to the Eagle Bluff Lighthouse parking area on the left. The trail starts adjacent to the entrance road. **Trailhead GPS:** N45 16.811' / W87 23.634'

The Hike

My list of all-time favorite hikes is long enough for a book of its own, and this hike ranks way up there, starting with drop-dead gorgeous views at the Eagle Bluff Lighthouse. Ogle the picture-perfect scene with a backdrop of Adventure, Little Strawberry, Jack, and Pirate Islands, and then pry yourself away to start the hike.

Follow the paved Sunset Trail along Shore Road and around Eagle Bluff, descending gradually past Nicolet Bay and then back up across the park road and into the woods. A right turn at Hidden Bluff Trail leads through more of the same ridiculously beautiful forest just south of the White Cedar Nature Reserve. The reserve's visitor center is nestled among the aroma of its namesake trees and is loaded with historic photos, park info, and gift items. This building was originally constructed in 1939 and was used as a warming house for the fearless crowd attempting the nearby ski jump and revelers at the toboggan run. Both sites were later abandoned, but the stories live on.

From the nature reserve and junction with Bluff Road, the trail descends easily to the water again and then along Tennison Bay to one final easy rise to the trailhead. Don't forget that the entire Sunset Trail is just over 9 miles and offers a full day of invigorating outdoor fun.

THE VERTICAL FOREST

The giant trees of the Pacific Northwest have some stiff competition in Wisconsin. The ancient white cedars growing in the "vertical forest" of Door County's Niagara Escarpment are grizzled and wise, latched onto solid rock for centuries. The stalwart trees sprouted from tiny fissures in sheer rock faces and escaped the ravages of logging, agriculture, and rampant development. At Ontario's Bruce Peninsula, a team of scientists discovered cedars just 10 feet tall and a foot in diameter that are more than 1,000 years old.

Sailing on Nicolet Bay DENICE BREAUX

Why Go?

Atop the park's 150-foot cliffs is a second growth maple-beech forest that once covered more than a third of Wisconsin. Clinging to the cliffs in seemingly gravity-defying form is a vertical forest of northern white cedars, some of which are more than 500 years old. Meadows with native grasses reside in place of original family farms, and the White Cedar Forest includes a rare succession of five distinct ecosystems that evolve with increasing elevation from the cold waters of Green Bay.

Miles and Directions

0.0 From the trailhead, set off hiking north on the Sunset Trail adjacent to Shore Road, and loop around Eagle Bluff.

0.1 Follow the Sunset Trail signs across the park road and continue past Nicolet Bay.

1.0 Cross Bluff Road and go right at Hidden Bluff Trail, hiking back toward the water.

2.7 Turn right at the Sunset Trail junction.

3.8 Arrive back at the trailhead.

Bay views through the trees DENICE BREAUX

22 Whitefish Dunes State Park

How's this for a day out? Nearly 900 acres of aged forest on 3 miles of rugged Lake Michigan shoreline and Wisconsin's highest sand dunes. Come out and roam.

Distance: 2.8 miles, with options for additional miles
Difficulty: Easy
Photogenic factor: 5
Hiking time: About 75 minutes
Trail surface: Hard-packed dirt and sand dunes
Other trail users: None
Canine compatibility: Leashed pets allowed

Land status: State park
Fees and permits: Vehicle pass required
Maps: Park maps; USGS Jacksonport
Trail contacts: Whitefish Dunes State Park, 3275 Clark Lake Rd., Sturgeon Bay, WI 54235; (920) 823-2400; dnr.wi.gov/topic/parks/name/whitefish

Finding the trailhead: From Sturgeon Bay, follow WI 42/57 north 2.7 miles to the split, and then WI 57 north 5.9 miles to Clark Lake Road. Turn right and follow Clark Lake Road 3.8 miles to the park entrance. The trailhead is adjacent to the nature center. **Trailhead GPS:** N44 92.724' / W87 18.297'

The Hike

Did you know that the land of today's Whitefish Dunes State Park has evidence of humans settling as far back as 100 BC? That's a long time ago, and other people settled here at no less than seven other time periods up to the late 1800s.

What drew consistent groups of people to this place? Most likely it was the great abundance of fish such as lake sturgeon, whitefish, walleye, and trout, as well as plants for food and medicine. Indeed, many rare plant species lived here in the earliest days and still do today, a fact that spurred 1930 conservationists to protect the dunes area from development.

And we are very glad they did because today one can walk along the peaceful quiet of the dunes and see tracks of foxes and deer or spot a muskrat or rabbit or even an elusive black bear. While most of the park's land-based wildlife only occasionally reveal themselves, scat, bones, and tracks are common sights.

Visitors are more likely to see and hear birds overhead and in the forested areas, grassy dunes, wetlands, and at the shoreline. And what an avian lineup it is, including the likes of Canada warbler, osprey, least flycatcher, black-throated blue and green warbler, and many others. Wetland areas are home to vibrant populations of amphibians such as wood frogs, spring peepers, chorus frogs, toads, salamanders, and turtles.

Flora at Whitefish is no less dramatic than the critters, with rare species such as thick-spike wheatgrass, prairie sand reed, and Wisconsin's largest population of the

Footprints in the sand along the shore DENICE BREAUX

threatened dune thistle. Vibrant flowers live here as well. On your hike look for dune goldenrod, dwarf lake iris, and sand reedgrass.

The beach, of course, is the big geographic draw, and like its enormous Saharan relative, the dunes at Whitefish are constantly in motion, forever at the mercy of nature's hand. Winds bellowing in from across Lake Michigan blast against the shore, lift up the sand grain by grain, and move it inland. This action eventually forms a dune. The wind then drops down the steep back slope of the dune, picks up more sand, and builds another dune.

The whole thing is like an eternal highlight reel of nature in action and makes this hike all the more enjoyable. The red trail takes hikers south from the nature center into the woods along the lakeshore. A couple of beach-access points take you to the water's edge and along the dunes. About halfway through the hike, you will reach the junction with the Old Baldy Trail. Don't miss this short side trip along a boardwalk and up a set of stairs to the park's highest point at 93 feet above lake level. There's an observation deck up there and outrageous views of Lake Michigan, Clark Lake, and a big chunk of the rest of the park.

From Baldy, the red trail mingles with the green and yellow trails back to the trailhead.

The cordwalk trail along the dunes above Lake Michigan KENT MERHAR

Lake Michigan shoreline and dunes DENICE BREAUX

Whitefish Dunes State Park

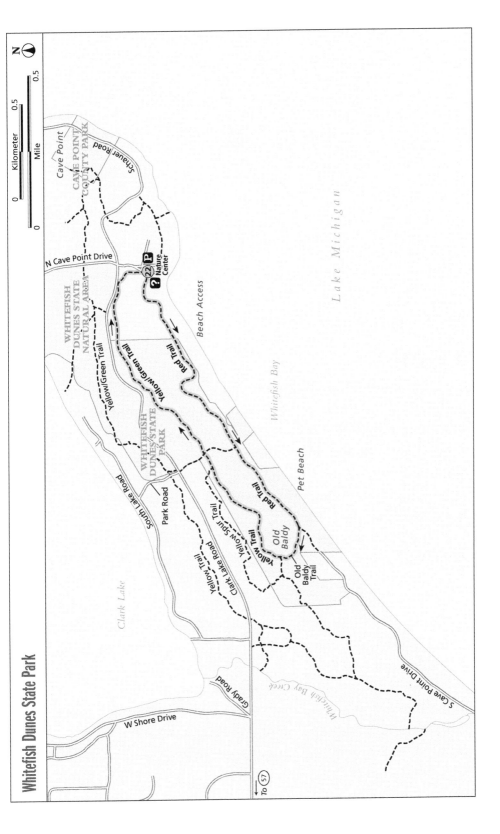

Why Go?

The Whitefish Dunes–Shivering Sands Important Bird Area (IBA) is a unique and wildlife-rich mix of sandy beaches, lowland cedar swamps, and ridges capped with dense forest. This is Wisconsin's most significant IBA and home to successional ecosystems and rare plants such as thick-spike wheat grass and the federally threatened dune thistle. Recent acquisition of additional property has bolstered the area's protection but timber harvest and development pressures are a constant threat.

Miles and Directions

0.0 From the trailhead, follow the red trail south from the nature center, almost immediately passing a beach-access trail.

0.7 Pass another beach-access trail.

1.3 At the junction with Old Baldy Trail, head up the spur trail and stairs for great views from the top. Loop back on the red trail, which mingles with the yellow and green, to return to the trailhead.

2.8 Arrive back at the trailhead.

DUNE PEOPLE

From 100 BC to AD 300 the Whitefish Dunes area was occupied by its earliest settlers, the North Bay people. Their territory extended from Green Bay to Rock Island, within which there were likely several separate but interacting bands who traveled the shores of the peninsula by canoe. These people were skilled in pottery craft, and archaeologists have discovered much evidence among the dunes. It is believed the North Bay people lived here only in the spring and summer, probably arriving for spring sturgeon fishing and staying to midsummer. Then what? Did they winter in Phoenix?

The Heins Creek people descended from the North Bay groups, occupying the shores of the Door Peninsula in a large population supported through fishing. The Heins Creek people lived here to about AD 750.

The next occupation were the Woodland people, from AD 800 to AD 900. By now, a good-sized village had been established and bustled with activity from spring to fall, with winter seeing the departure of the population to winter hunting camps on the Green Bay side or inland wetland areas.

The Oneota people arrived in this area around AD 900 and were likely descendants of the later Woodland groups. The Oneota introduced agriculture to their lives, in addition to traditional hunting and fishing. Corn and squash were popular, the former probably ground to flour to make dough. One archaeological dig uncovered a pit oven with fire-hardened dolomite.

23 Potawatomi State Park

One of Wisconsin's state park gems, Potawatomi boasts rolling, emerald-green valleys complemented by raggedy limestone cliffs and ridiculously gorgeous views of Sturgeon Bay.

Distance: 2.6 miles, with options for additional miles
Difficulty: Easy
Photogenic factor: 5
Hiking time: About 75 minutes
Trail surface: Hard-packed dirt
Other trail users: None
Canine compatibility: Leashed pets allowed

Land status: State park
Fees and permits: Vehicle pass required
Maps: Park maps; USGS Sturgeon Bay West
Trail contacts: Potawatomi State Park, 3740 CR PD, Sturgeon Bay, WI 54235; (920) 746-2890; dnr.wi.gov/topic/parks/name/potawatomi

Finding the trailhead: From Green Bay at I-43, follow WI 57 north 36 miles to Park Drive (CR PD). Turn left (north) and head 2.4 miles to the park entrance. From the entrance station, follow South Norway Road 1 mile to a parking area on the right. Find the trail at the north end. **Trailhead GPS:** N44 85.377' / W87 40.387'

The Hike

When I am at this magical place, I always feel a deep sense of vicarious pride and often walk with thoughts drifting to a time long past. The American Indian tribe who once called this land home were known as Bo-De-Wad-Me—"keeper of the fire." They lived in a land of rugged cliffs and forests high above the bay; among the gulls and terns, songbirds and deer.

The state park we see today retains much of that mystique and spirit. Dense forest of maple, birch, basswood, and red and white pine blanket a blend of sweeping valleys and short rocky hills and knobs. Among the trees live a host of wild critters. White-tailed deer are all over, along with foxes, squirrels, raccoons, turtles, and waterfowl. Well over 200 species of songbirds of various ilk live in or migrate through the park, and you can see herring gulls, ring-billed gulls, and terns riding the thermals along the cliffside shoreline.

This hike along the Hemlock Trail takes in much of those highlights, starting right off the bat by sharing double billing with the Ice Age Trail (IAT) along the cliff top above Sturgeon Bay. In fact, the IAT's eastern terminus is just a short way south of this hike's starting point. Views of the bay appear through intermittent breaks in the trees and soon you are treated to a linger-worthy overlook of Cabot Point, the mainland far across the bay, and faraway views of Green Bay to the northwest. Unforgettable.

The rustic Hemlock Trail DENICE BREAUX

Near Hills Point the path crosses the park road and makes a short, steep climb away from the water and into thick woods. In a short bit the IAT splits off and continues northwest while the Hemlock Trail takes a gradual curve past the campground area and nature center.

Cross the road again and begin heading due south, paralleling the road to your left. The trail stays mostly flat along this section, crosses the road once again, and then travels over barely there hills to a final downhill coast to the trailhead.

Got some extra time? The Ancient Shorelines Nature Trail is a don't-miss park highlight, and the Tower Trail treats hikers to its namesake, 75-foot observation tower with a 180-degree view of Sawyer Harbor. On clear days you can see 16 miles across Green Bay. Nice! And don't forget about the park's pair of campgrounds with well

DOOR COUNTY'S STONE FLEET

Door County's first industry, a limestone quarry, started in 1834 at Government Bluff, 150 feet above Sturgeon Bay. The original plan was to use the stone to build a military fort, but that never came to pass. The federal government, however, used the stone to build piers and harbors around Lake Michigan. By 1898 four more quarries were built and supplied stone to construct nearly every pier and breakwater around the lake.

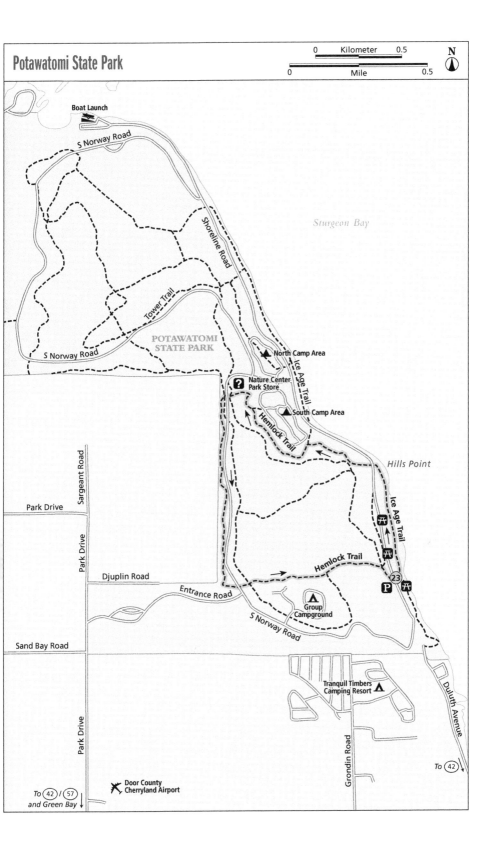

Potawatomi State Park

0 Kilometer 0.5
0 Mile 0.5

N

Boat Launch

S Norway Road

Shoreline Road

Sturgeon Bay

Tower Trail

POTAWATOMI
STATE PARK

S Norway Road

North Camp Area

Ice Age Trail

Nature Center
Park Store

South Camp Area

Hemlock Trail

Hills Point

Ice Age Trail

Sargeant Road

Park Drive

Park Drive

Djuplin Road

Hemlock Trail

Entrance Road

23

P

S Norway Road

Group
Campground

Sand Bay Road

Tranquil Timbers
Camping Resort

Duluth Avenue

Park Drive

Grondin Road

To 42

Door County
Cherryland Airport

To 42 / 57
and Green Bay

Dreamy views of Sturgeon Bay DENICE BREAUX

over one hundred campsites. Winter camping (brrrr) is popular here as well, as is cross-country skiing, sledding, and snowshoeing.

Why Go?

Door County holds high ground in the pantheon of extraordinary places, here in Wisconsin and across the country. Potawatomi's coastal ecosystem complements those all over the county, including The Ridges Sanctuary in Baileys Harbor. Founded in 1937 to protect a 30-acre parcel along the northwest shore of the harbor, The Ridges Sanctuary continues education and research efforts to nurture the state's most biologically diverse ecosystem.

Miles and Directions

0.0 From the trailhead, set off hiking northbound along the shoreline.

0.8 Reach the Hills Point area. Cross the park road and continue on the trail into the woods.

1.0 Ice Age Trail splits here and continues northwest. Veer left and follow the Heritage Trail past the campground area and nature center.

1.4 Cross the road again, curve left, and hike due south, paralleling the road.

2.3 Reach another road crossing and head downhill.

2.6 Arrive back at the trailhead.

All we need is love DENICE BREAUX

24 Point Beach State Forest

With six miles of Lake Michigan beach, 11 miles of hiking trails, and an active US Coast Guard lighthouse, this loop traces the shoreline and an ancient dune ridge.

Distance: 4.6 miles, with options for additional miles	**Canine compatibility:** Leashed pets allowed
Difficulty: Easy	**Land status:** State forest
Photogenic factor: 5	**Fees and permits:** Vehicle pass required
Hiking time: About 1 hour and 45 minutes	**Maps:** Park maps; USGS Two Rivers
Trail surface: Hard-packed dirt	**Trail contacts:** Point Beach State Forest, 9400 CR O, Two Rivers, WI 54241; (920) 794-7480; dnr.wi.gov/topic/parks/name/pointbeach
Other trail users: Mountain bikers	

Finding the trailhead: From WI 42 in Two Rivers, follow CR O 4.7 miles north to the park entrance road. Follow this road 0.3 mile to the parking area and trailhead. **Trailhead GPS:** N44 21.132' / W87 50.990'

The Hike

After the time of American Indian residence here during the Copper Culture age, including Winnebago, Sauk, Fox, Miami, and Potawatomi people, a settler named Peter Rowley moved in and set up a trading post. He decided to name the place Mink River, but when surveyors scouted the area in the mid-1800s, they had never heard of the Mink River name. They knew of Rowley, however, and renamed the location after him (changing the spelling a few years later to Rawley Point).

A robust hemlock population here spurred the establishment of many tanneries, such as the Wisconsin Leather Company. Hemlock is a main ingredient for making leather, and for close to four decades this was the highlight industry in the Two Rivers area.

Much of the end product from the leather trade was transported by steamers and schooners, and Lake Michigan's waters were busy with vessels navigating its challenging waters. Some ships unfortunately didn't make it to the next port. Shipwrecks are common throughout the Great Lakes, and one of Lake Michigan's most notable

FINAL VOYAGE

On January 15, 1885, the tug *Boss* was moored securely to a dock in Two Rivers. The next morning it was missing. A fierce winter storm was in the works and many people thought the tug broke its lines and drifted out into the lake. Others guessed it was cast adrift or even stolen. The tug was found in the spring of 1887 about 4 miles south of Two Rivers.

Shoreside Lake Michigan views DENICE BREAUX

was the steamer *Vernon*, which sank 200 feet down in an area less than a dozen miles northeast of Two Rivers. The ship settled upright on the lake bottom and remains upright today, making it a huge hit with divers.

Another famous wreck was the *Rouse Simmons*, popularly known as the Christmas Tree Ship. Every year, two brothers from Michigan filled the *Rouse* with Christmas trees to bring to Chicago. Alas, the ship disappeared in a harsh 1912 storm and only a few washed-ashore trees remained until a diver discovered the wreck in 1971, still packed with hundreds of trees with their needles perfectly preserved. Reports differ on why the ship sank but some put the onus on the enormous load of trees that didn't allow the ship to ride at an optimal level.

Terrestrial-based features of Point Beach State Forest include its three State Natural Areas (SNAs). Wilderness Ridge SNA is dominated by a ridge-swale environment with nearly thirty species of sedges and dozens more of grasses. Two Creeks Buried Forest SNA is just north of the state forest and includes 11,000-year-old sediment layers. Point Beach Ridges SNA is home to swales and ridges and the endangered sand dune willow.

Start this hike from the lighthouse area and head south on the Ice Age Trail. The trail meanders south, alternating between the beach and a grove of white cedar woods, with a couple of enticing boardwalk access trails and beachside benches. The trail passes directly over the dunes, with sights and sounds of Lake Michigan right off your left shoulder. Hike past the indoor group camp cabins, and in short order Molash Creek appears beyond the pines, with a bench conveniently located for viewing this idyllic scene.

Boardwalk trail toward the lake DENICE BREAUX

Hiking a wide trail in the woods DENICE BREAUX

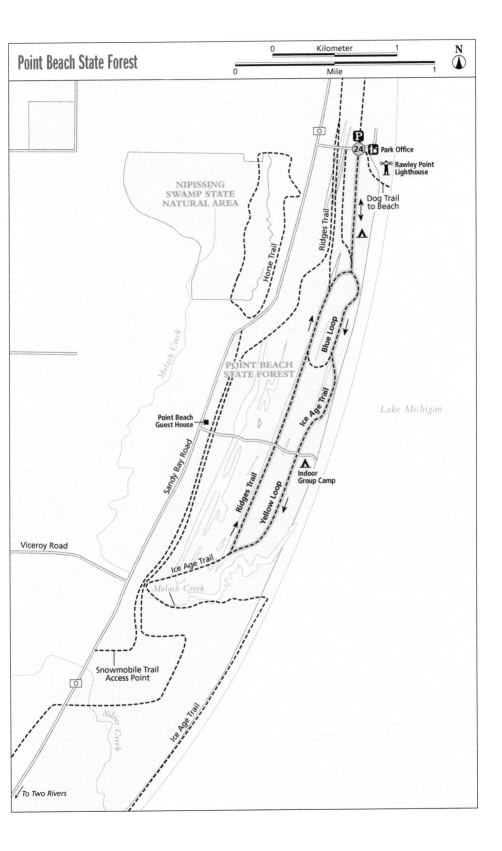

Point Beach State Forest

0 Kilometer 1
0 Mile 1

N

Park Office
Rawley Point Lighthouse
Dog Trail to Beach

NIPISSING SWAMP STATE NATURAL AREA

Horse Trail
Ridges Trail
Blue Loop
Ice Age Trail

POINT BEACH STATE FOREST

Lake Michigan

Point Beach Guest House

Sandy Bay Road

Ridges Trail
Yellow Loop
Indoor Group Camp

Viceroy Road

Ice Age Trail

Molash Creek

Snowmobile Trail Access Point

Silver Creek

Ice Age Trail

To Two Rivers

From here, connect with the Ridges Trail. This section of the hike makes a beeline back northeast through resplendent forest of maple, ash, beech, birch, aspen, red and white pine, and scattered hemlock.

Before long the path connects with the blue loop and returns to the trailhead.

Why Go?

Did you know that this small forest–dune environment includes nearly thirty species of sedges unique to Wisconsin? Nearby Two Creeks Buried Forest SNA also contains sediment layers dating to more than 11,000 years ago. Best of all, the ridges and swales of the dune ecosystem is our state's only known habitat of the endangered sand dune willow, as well as rare bird species such as the pine warbler, hooded warbler, and Acadian flycatcher.

Miles and Directions

0.0 From the trailhead near the lighthouse, hike due south on the trail adjacent to parking area's entrance. This will connect to the Ice Age Trail (IAT). Follow the IAT southbound along the shore, with Lake Michigan views on one side and lumpy dunes on the other.

2.5 Reach the junction with the Ridges Trail, turn right.

3.8 Turn right here for the final few dozen steps on the blue loop. Turn left (north) on the IAT and proceed straight ahead on the trail back to the trailhead.

4.6 Arrive back at the trailhead.

25 High Cliff State Park

Get elevated, drop-dead gorgeous views of Wisconsin's largest inland lake on this feature-packed hike, including Indian mounds and old lime kiln ruins.

Distance: 2.2 miles, with many options for additional mileage
Difficulty: Easy
Photogenic factor: 4+
Hiking time: About 90 minutes
Trail surface: Hard-packed dirt
Other trail users: None
Canine compatibility: Leashed pets allowed

Land status: State park
Fees and permits: Vehicle pass required
Maps: Park maps; USGS Sherwood
Trail contacts: High Cliff State Park, N7630 State Park Rd., Sherwood, WI 54169; (920) 989-1106; dnr.wi.gov/topic/parks/name/highcliff

Finding the trailhead: From the eastern fringe of the little town of Sherwood at WI 55, follow Clifton Road (becomes Spring Hill Drive) 1.6 miles to the park entrance. Past the entrance, turn left at Lower Cliff Road and go 0.7 mile to High Cliff Road. Turn left again and follow this road 0.7 mile to the last parking area on your left. The Red Bird Trail starts at the western end of the lot. **Trailhead GPS:** N44 16.283' / W88 28.669'

The Hike

Lake Winnebago is the largest lake within Wisconsin's borders, stretching 31 miles north to south and roughly 7 miles east to west. It's a big ol' lake and attracts legions of water-loving fans on all manner of watercraft. It also offers great views of the rugged limestone cliffs rising 40 feet above the eastern shore, making up part of the Niagara Escarpment; the immense limestone band stretching from Wisconsin to its namesake falls in New York. This fascinating geological wonder is made of countless layers of limestone sediment deposited here millions of years ago. High Cliff State Park boasts more than a mile of wildly scenic shoreline (with its own marina), and is home to red foxes, deer, woodchucks, warblers, and an active population of purple martins.

The park is also steeped in human history, dating back 1,500 years to nomadic people who built still-visible effigy mounds in the shapes of animals (such as panthers, buffalo, and bears) or geometric shapes (including conical and lineal). The much more recent years of the late 1800s to mid-1900s were very lively times in the company town of Clifton, made up of worker housing, a store, a telegraph office, and, of course, a tavern. The Western Lime and Cement Company owned the town, and product extracted from the quarry was shipped all over the Midwest for use in cement, brick mortar, and gravel. Today the old store is a museum where visitors can see the kiln ruins and hike the historic Lime Kiln Trail.

Gorgeous view of Lake Winnebago DENICE BREAUX

For a highlight reel of the park's best, beeline to the Red Bird Trail, marked at the trailhead with an impressive statue of Red Bird, a Winnebago tribe leader and peacemaker with early settlers. Close to the statue is another area landmark: a wooden observation tower that takes you 40 feet in the air for outrageous views of the lake and bucolic Wisconsin countryside.

Start this unforgettable hike heading southwest along the top of the escarpment, past the magnificent statue of Chief Red Bird. The first sections of the hike are mostly level, with just a few gentle rollers. You'll score stellar views of the big lake from up here along the escarpment, from overlooks through the stunning forest of maple, elm, and some aspen. Across the park road, the trail passes by an old limestone quarry site and down to the Indian mounds area. I always linger a little in places like this, in part to pay silent respect and to soak in the palpable vibe of a fascinating remnant of a people who made their home here.

THE GENERAL STORE

Hearken back to the bustling mid-1800s town of High Cliff. The little burg bustled with activity from the lime quarry, and in the midst of it all was the General Store. Built from bricks made on-site, the cozy building served as a store, post office, telegraph office, and Western Lime and Cement's office. The store was the quintessential small-town gathering place to meet neighbors, tip a hat to a lady, or just settle into a chair on the porch and watch the goings-on of the day. The building today hosts a museum packed with historical photos and relics from the town's mining heyday.

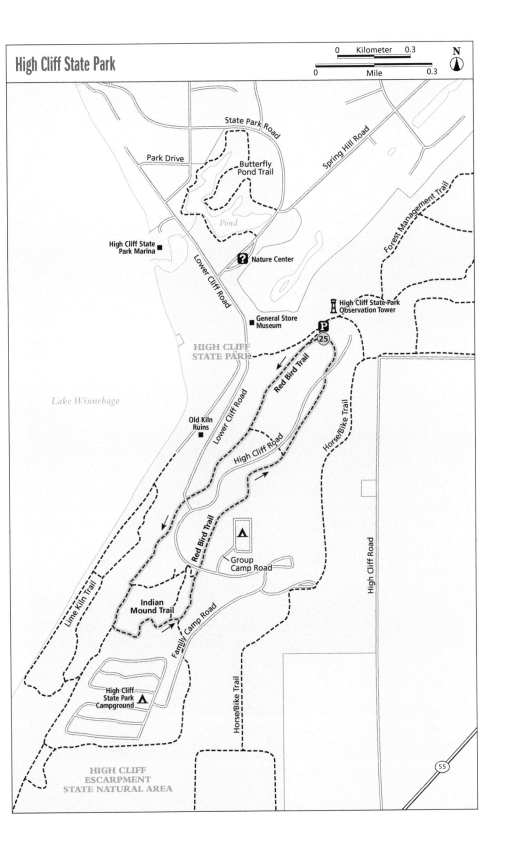

High Cliff State Park

Beauteous views of the lake and shoreline DENICE BREAUX

Trail through dense forest DENICE BREAUX

From the Indian mounds, hang a left and head up a substantial climb past a group of enormous old cottonwoods to the top of the ridge. From here, the Red Bird Trail rolls up and down a series of little valleys back north through the woods to the park road and trailhead.

Why Go?

The High Cliff Escarpment State Natural Area is highlighted by the unique cliff habitats, a long stretch of lake shoreline and enormous numbers of migrating birds in spring and fall. Several purple martin colonies reside here, and this is one of Wisconsin's go-to locations to see the spring warbler migration. High Cliff also boasts a colorful, melodious cast of rare species, including winter wren, snow bunting, orchard oriole, upland sandpiper, and others.

Miles and Directions

0.0 Hike the Red Bird Trail southwest from the trailhead, along the escarpment.

0.6 Cross the park road.

0.9 Reach the escarpment natural area and Indian mounds, turn left.

1.2 Pass one trail junction and turn left at the next, heading back north on the Red Bird Trail. (Both junctions offer options for additional trail mileage.)

2.0 Reach junction with park road, hike along it back to the parking area and trailhead.

2.2 Arrive back at the trailhead.

26 Kohler-Andrae State Park

This popular state park is one of Lake Michigan's last natural preserves, boasting 2 miles of sandy beach, trails through majestic dunes, and rare interdunal wetlands.

Distance: 2.6 miles
Difficulty: Moderate
Photogenic factor: 5
Hiking time: About 90 minutes
Trail surface: Wooden cordwalk
Other trail users: None
Canine compatibility: Leashed pets allowed north of the nature center only

Land status: State park
Fees and permits: Vehicle pass required
Maps: Park maps; USGS Sheboygan South
Trail contacts: Kohler-Andrae State Park, 1020 Beach Park Ln., Sheboygan, WI 53081; (920) 451-4080; dnr.wi.gov/topic/parks/name/kohlerandrae

Finding the trailhead: From Sheboygan, follow I-43 south to exit 120 (CR V). Follow CR V east 2 miles to its junction with Beach Park Lane and continue straight ahead into the park. Just past the park entrance, turn left and follow Beach Park Lane 0.3 mile to the trailhead. **Trailhead GPS:** N43 67.247' / W87 71.315'

The Hike

Even if you don't hail from the Sheboygan area, you are likely familiar with the Kohler name—if nothing else, simply from standing over a kitchen sink or sitting on a toilet. John Michael Kohler emigrated to the US in 1854 and worked at his father-in-law's machine shop, later turning "Kohler" into a household name. Since 1914 the Kohler Company has supplied our country with all manner of plumbing fixtures and today is the nation's second largest in the industry. Mr. Kohler contributed generously to the community and his company donated a large land parcel on the shores of Lake Michigan, which eventually became John Michael Kohler State Park.

Perhaps less known to you is the Terry Andrae name. Mr. Andrae presided over a Milwaukee-based electric company, and in 1924 bought 122 acres of lakeshore property. He built a lodge there with his wife and made great efforts to preserve and improve the pine forest and dunes. When Andrae died in 1927, his wife Elsbeth donated the land to the state and Terry Andrae State Park was formed.

Additional land was added to the parcels and today both parks are managed as one unit, and what a place it is! The park is packed with a lively array of flora and fauna, from the water to the dunes to the forest. White-tailed deer are common here, of course, as are red foxes, muskrats, and coyotes. More prevalent are at least 150 species of birds living in or visiting the area. The shoreline is a busy migration corridor in spring and fall and we are treated to raucous crowds of diving ducks, hawks, gulls, warblers, vireos, cranes, and herons. It's a bevy of birdwatching!

The cordwalk through the trees KENT MERHAR

The cordwalk through a meadow KENT MERHAR

Not only that, Kohler-Andrae boasts more than 400 plant and 50 tree species, many of which are found only here. And don't miss the Kohler Park Dunes State Natural Area to spot one-of-a-kind dune vegetation and other threatened species.

This is a mostly linear path, wholly within Kohler Park Dunes State Natural Area, with a loop in the middle. From the trailhead at the far northern end of the park, hike south on the cordwalk. These ingenious walkways allow up-close access to this fascinating and fragile ecosystem. The trail passes through a small copse of pines, past a little loop, and then rolls along and through and over compact meadows filled with a mix of ground-level foliage and short, weather-hardened trees. Some of these dune hollows remind me of enormous golf course sand traps adorned with grasses and shrubbery.

The scenery escapes worthy superlatives; you'll know what I mean when you hike here. One minute you're ogling faraway views of Lake Michigan's blue expanse and the next you're passing by a soaring sand dune with whiskers of seagrass rustling in the breeze. What a truly special place to be part of, don't you think?

WHAT'S AN INTERDUNAL WETLAND?

Sand dunes are fascinating displays of nature's creativity, and dunes around the Great Lakes take it a step further. Nestled within open dunes or between beach ridges are wetland areas dominated with sedges, rushes, and shrubs, featuring a fluctuating water table in sync with changes in the lake level. Water in these areas warms much faster than the big lakes and provides critical feeding stops for migrating birds and forage for waterfowl such as spotted sandpipers, piping plovers, and great blue herons. Dragonflies, midges, damselflies, and many other invertebrates love it here, too.

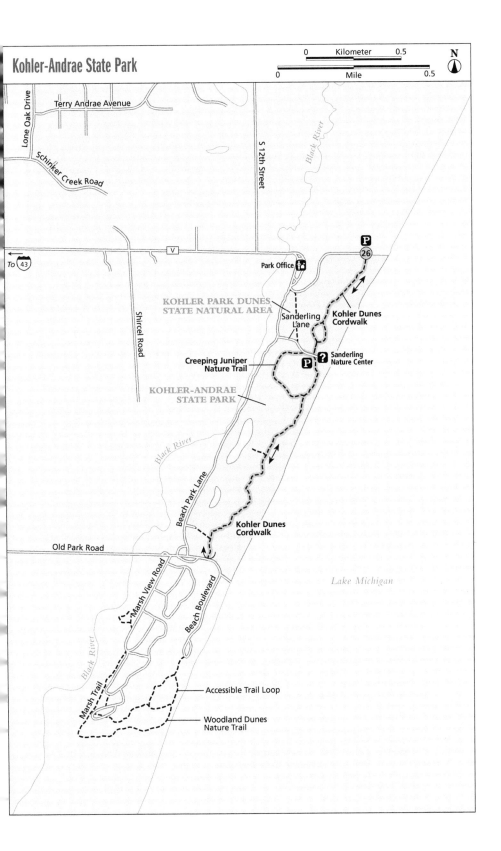

Kohler-Andrae State Park

0   Kilometer   0.5
0   Mile   0.5

N

Lone Oak Drive

Terry Andrae Avenue

Schinker Creek Road

S 12th Street

Black River

V

To 43

Park Office

P
26

KOHLER PARK DUNES
STATE NATURAL AREA

Sanderling
L'ane

Kohler Dunes
Cordwalk

Shircel Road

Creeping Juniper
Nature Trail

P

Sanderling
Nature Center

KOHLER-ANDRAE
STATE PARK

Black River

Beach Park Lane

Kohler Dunes
Cordwalk

Old Park Road

Lake Michigan

Marsh View Road

Beach Boulevard

Black River

Marsh Trail

Accessible Trail Loop

Woodland Dunes
Nature Trail

Dune accoutrements KENT MERHAR

Past Sanderling Nature Center, a pair of short spur trails lead to the beach for ample opportunity to mingle with the waves, amble the shoreline, or build a sandcastle. Stop in at the Sanderling Nature Center for intriguing displays and interpretive intel on the dune area, and then continue a winding and rolling course on the cordwalk, passing a few more beach-access trails along the way until arriving at the turnaround point at Old Park Road. On the return, turn left at the junction just south of the nature center to complete the mid-hike loop.

Why Go?

Some of the Great Lakes' last remnants of natural dunes are found along Lake Michigan's shores at Kohler Park Dunes State Natural Area, part of Kohler-Andrae State Park. This vibrantly scenic place provides critical habitat for many threatened and endangered plant species, including pitcher's thistle, clustered broomrape, sand reedgrass, and thistle spike. Dedicated efforts of local and state groups are doing great things to preserve this precious space.

Miles and Directions

0.0 Hike south from the trailhead, following the cordwalk.

0.3 Choose right or left at this junction (both ways meet on the other side).

0.4 Veer left through the nature center parking lot and pick up the trail about halfway down on the lake side.

0.6 Take the left fork, staying on a southerly track, passing spur trails to the beach on your left..

1.3 The trail ends at Old Park Road. About-face to return to the trailhead. Turn left at the junction just south of the nature center to complete the mid-hike loop.

2.6 Arrive back at the trailhead.

27 Lion's Den Gorge

Score some of Lake Michigan's best views on this flat, ridgetop trail along one of the lake's last stretches of undeveloped shoreline.

Distance: 1.9 miles, with options for additional miles
Difficulty: Easy
Photogenic factor: 5
Hiking time: About 1 hour
Trail surface: Gravel, dirt, and boardwalk
Other trail users: None

Canine compatibility: Leashed pets allowed
Land status: Ozaukee County
Fees and permits: None
Maps: Park maps; USGS Cedarburg
Trail contacts: Ozaukee County Parks, 121 Main St., Port Washington, WI 53074; (262) 284-9411, co.ozaukee.wi.us

Finding the trailhead: From I-43, take the CR Q/WI 60 exit and head east on CR Q (Ulao Road) 0.9 mile to CR C. Turn left and follow CR C 1.8 miles to High Bluff Drive and turn right. The trailhead is 0.3 mile on the left. **Trailhead GPS:** N43 20.168' / W87 53.225'

The Hike

Good on ya, Ozaukee County. In rare dedication to steering away from development, county officials chose to establish Lion's Den Gorge as a nature preserve with a bow toward ecology. It worked so well that the area quickly became a model for planning and creating other preserves in the county. And what a place to start—Lion's Den is situated on about a mile of blissfully undeveloped bluff land and Lake Michigan shoreline, purchased from a like-minded private landowner. Since then, the park has attracted legions of visitors and area students to its straight-up gorgeous beauty and unique educational stage, including an adjacent natural area untouched since times prior to European settlement.

With your first steps on this hike, you'll agree it is truly a gem in Wisconsin's crown of extraordinary places. Sandstone bluffs 100 feet above the lake offer amazing views across the water, and on clear days you can see the historic Port Washington lighthouse nearly 3 miles to the north. The park is small, at just 73 acres, but over-flowing with enough scenic wonders to fill a day out and then some. The trails pass through a mix of white cedar and hardwood forest, grassland, wet meadows, and the rugged gorge. This diversity nurtures a vibrant population of resident wildlife and native wildflowers, and the trails feature wooden boardwalks in some sections, bridges over the gorge, stairway access to a beach, and bonus hiking at the neighboring Ulao Waterfowl Production Area. The high bluff is, of course, the perfect place to sit back and watch the spring and fall hawk migrations. Many other birds are common here as well, including more than twenty warbler species, green heron, rails, least bittern, pie-billed grebe, and wood ducks.

Wide, curvy scenery (left); the Gorge bridge (right) KENT MERHAR

From the west trailhead, set off on the Waterfowl Walk Trail past the southern edge of the Ulao property and head for the Bluff Trail. A vista overlook serves up phenomenal views right off the bat and you can soak in more of them for awhile before the path leads into the dense, shady woods. (Junctions with Woodland Way and Wetland Way offer options for different loops and more or less mileage.) Don't miss the short spur trail to another overlook and stay the course on Bluff Trail through the trees all the way to a bridge crossing the gorge. A gorge overlook provides yet another ideal vantage point to ogle the grand lake views. Cross the wooden bridge to a stairway down to the beach. Don't forget your swimsuit; the lake is a welcome refresher on a steamy hot summer day.

Once you've had your fill of beach time, head back up to the trail, but this time turn right on the Gorge Loop Trail, curve around the top of the loop, and follow an arrow-straight course on the Lion's Den Trail back to the trailhead.

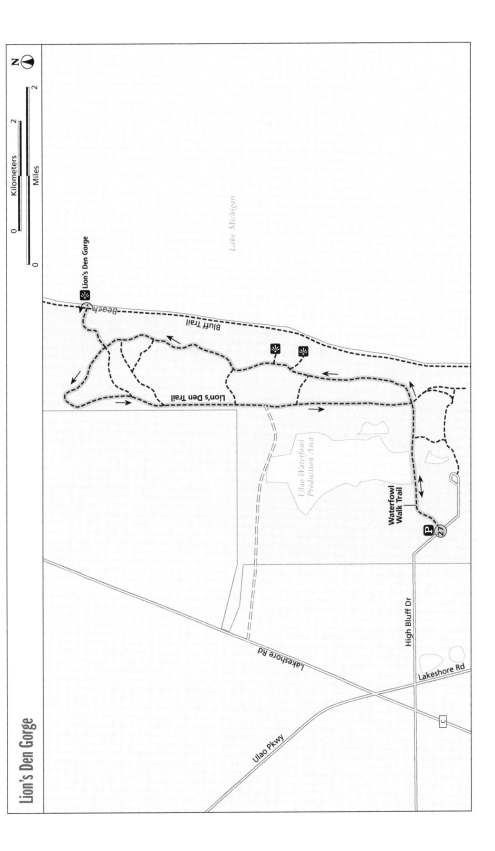

Boardwalk toward the lake KENT MERHAR

Why Go?

Hugging the western edge of the preserve is the Ulao Waterfowl Production Area, a U.S. Fish and Wildlife Service and Leopold Wetland Management District property focused on "enhancing populations of migratory birds and other wildlife." Don't miss a hike through the area to see loons, scoters, dozens of species of ducks and brethren water birds, and songbirds such as the northern mockingbird, orchard oriole, and warblers.

Miles and Directions

0.0 Follow Waterfowl Walk Trail north toward the Bluff Trail.

0.2 Reach junction with the Bluff Trail and continue north.

0.4 Reach junction with Woodland Way; turn right on Bluff Trail.

0.5 Take a right on the short out-and-back spur trail to an overlook.

0.6 Turn right at Wetland Way to stay on Bluff Trail.

0.8 Arrive at Gorge Vista and the bridge. Head across to access the beach via stairs.

0.9 Head back up the stairs and veer right at Gorge Vista onto the Gorge Loop.

1.2 Connect with the Lion's Den Trail for the return to the trailhead.

1.9 Arrive back at the trailhead.

28 Milwaukee Lakefront Trail

Milwaukee's lakefront is alive with no end of things to do, from museums to art galleries to unique eateries. This hike follows part of the Oak Leaf Trail on a loping course through the heart of it all.

Distance: 3-mile lollipop, with options for many additional miles
Difficulty: Easy
Photogenic factor: 5
Hiking time: About 90 minutes
Trail surface: Paved
Other trail users: Bicyclists, runners, skaters

Canine compatibility: Leashed pets allowed
Land status: County park
Fees and permits: None
Maps: Park maps; USGS South Milwaukee
Trail contacts: Milwaukee County Parks, 9480 Watertown Rd., Wauwatosa, WI 53226; (414) 257-7275; county.milwaukee.gov

Finding the trailhead: From I-43, exit at North Avenue and follow it east 2.2 miles to North Terrace Avenue. Turn left (north) and a quick right on East Water Tower Road and follow it 0.3 mile to North Lincoln Memorial Drive. Head straight across to the parking area and trailhead. **Trailhead GPS:** N43 05.775' / W87 87.698'

The Hike

In a rare but admirable and much-celebrated effort, the city of Milwaukee long ago chose to underutilize its prized lakefront, sparing it from the ravages of overdevelopment and instead keeping the area natural for all of us to enjoy. Salud!

Laced throughout the metro area is the Oak Leaf Trail, the umbrella name for the city's prized 125-mile trail system, with dozens of trailheads that provide access to most anywhere in the city. The Lakefront Trail segment, stretching from the University of Wisconsin-Milwaukee at the north end to South Milwaukee, hugs the Lake Michigan shoreline and takes in the Milwaukee Art Museum, Veterans Park, McKinley Marina, the Summerfest grounds, and Bradford Beach at the north end.

WORLD'S LARGEST MUSIC FESTIVAL

That's a bold claim, but Milwaukee's Summerfest backs it up with an official Guinness Book of World Records designation. Since 1968 Summerfest has infused the Milwaukee lakefront with eleven days of lively music of nearly every genre from contemporary to gospel to hard rock and reggae. It's a big, big deal, attracting nearly 1 million people every year. All those fans have plenty from which to choose, with more than 1,000 performances taking place on twelve separate stages.

Bring your picnic basket Kent Merhar

Indeed, this is the place to be in sunny summer months, where Veterans Park introduces the city to the lake. Here you'll find all kinds of lively events, including kite festivals, Brewfest, the Air and Water Show, and lots of great live music. Looking for a place to stay? Check in at the historically classy Knickerbocker Hotel, and when you're hungry, head to some of the city's choicest dining destinations, such as Bartolotta's Lake Park Bistro. And don't miss the opportunity to tour Milwaukee's vintage East Side neighborhoods and the impeccably preserved North Point Lighthouse, built in 1888 and one of the city's oldest standing structures.

From the trailhead, start hiking southbound, and in short order pass McKinley Beach and its namesake marina. The marina boasts 600 boat slips packed with vessels of all shapes and sizes. Fishing charters ship off from here, or you can take a sailing lesson or rent a Jet Ski to buzz around on the bay.

A bit farther on, the trail reaches Lagoon Drive and skirts the west side of the lagoon down to the iconic Milwaukee Art Museum area. Here you will loop back north through Veterans Park to reconnect with the stem of this hike route for the homestretch back to the trailhead.

Conveniently enough, just north of the trailhead is Bradford Beach, the perfect place to unwind after your hike. Kick back in the sand, cool off with a swim, and, whatever you do, don't miss a stop at the custard stand for delectable desserts.

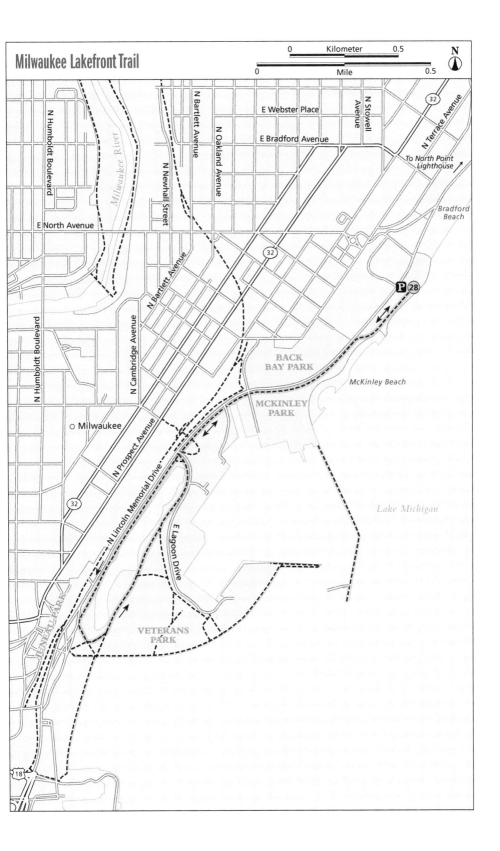

Beachside view of Milwaukee skyline KENT MERHAR

Why Go?

Complementing the cover shot–worthy scenery at every turn, nearby Lakeside State Park is a popular launch pad for all manner of outdoor activities with simultaneous views of Lake Michigan and Milwaukee's skyline. One of my favorite outings is piloting a bike on the Oak Leaf Trail, more than 125 miles of paved pathways that lace around the city, with a substantial portion following the breezy lake shoreline.

Miles and Directions

0.0   From the trailhead, hike south on the Oak Leaf Trail.

0.3   Pass McKinley Beach.

0.8   Cross East Lagoon Drive and the big marina.

1.5   Reach the General Douglas MacArthur statue near Veteran's Park and loop back north on the other side of the lagoon.

2.1   Reconnect with the stem of the trail at East Lagoon Drive and hike north.

3.0   Arrive back at the trailhead.

Central Wisconsin and Western Border

Wisconsin has a long and storied relationship with glaciers. Think moraines and kettles, knobs and swales, remnants of unfathomable power of millennia-long sculpt, retreat, repeat processes that created Wisconsin's central environs, an enchanting blend of rolling hills, transition forest, and wildly diverse ecosystems. Hikers in this region are treated to ancient ridgelines and trails that lope from rounded hills to shallow valleys. Rare plant species are, ironically, commonly seen and a celebrity list of wildlife wander the woods, bogs, and lakeshores, or fly the sky overhead. Some of my go-to hiking destinations include the Tolkien-esque Plum Lake Hemlock Forest, the century-old forest on the Straight Lake Trail; hilltop lakes along the Chippewa Moraine; the steeps at Brady's Bluff; and the soul-deep wild that is the Chequamegon.

Wisconsin's western border harbors some of America's most sublime countryside. The incomparable Driftless Area, or Coulee Region, is our own magic kingdom chock full of adventure. Complementing the bluff country, checkerboard farmland unfurls over rolling hills; easygoing rivers make lazy curves and oxbows, with accents of riffles and rapids; and placid glacial lakes tuck below high ridgelines. Unforgettable hiking options are as free and liberating as a daydream—wander through historic American Indian lineage and stroll relaxing trails along the Kinnickinnic Gorge and St. Croix River; go steep in the lumpy bluffs of Perrot State Park, climb to Wisconsin's highest point, or unwind at Wyalusing.

29 Falls Bluff Loop-Osceola

Bring the kids and follow historic routes of American Indians and early settlers on this short and scenic hike amidst St. Croix River bluffs.

Distance: 1.2 miles, with options for additional miles
Difficulty: Easy to moderate with one steep climb
Photogenic factor: 4
Hiking time: 45 minutes
Trail surface: Hard-packed dirt
Other trail users: None

Canine compatibility: Leashed pets allowed
Land status: City of Osceola
Fees and permits: None
Maps: Osceola city maps; USGS Osceola
Trail contacts: Osceola Area Chamber, PO Box 251, Osceola, WI 54020; (715) 755-3300; myosceolachamber.org

Finding the trailhead: Look for the statue of Chief Osceola on the west side of North Cascade Street near the Wisconsin Milk House, about 1 block north of Highway 243. **Trailhead GPS:** N45 31.981' / W92 70.604'

The Hike

A visit to Osceola's charming downtown is always a treat, with its National Historic Site main street, and St. Croix River only steps away. The fun little town has been part of my travels since childhood and in an amusing aside, thanks to regular road construction detours over the years, Osceola adopted a self-proclaimed slogan as "The best small town you never meant to visit." It really is a fun and picturesque place and, best of all, offers multiple hiking trails that lead to a hidden river glen, waterfall, and a challenging climb to beautiful views of the river valley. Next time you're driving through, or looking for an exhilarating, uber-scenic day out, don't miss this loop. An amalgamation of the Simenstad, Eagle Bluff, and Cascade Falls Trails, the Falls Bluff Loop follows aged routes of Chippewa and Sioux people and channels the town's historic mill lineage.

Small bands of Sioux people first lived in the area, forced out later by Chippewa, and Seminole people also had a presence here, led by Chief Osceola. LeRoy Hubbard was the first white settler in the area, followed by many others, and in 1844, Cascade Falls was discovered on its namesake creek. The falls offered consistent, robust power, and flour, lumber, and grist mill industries grew up around it. The small village that blossomed was first named LeRoy in Mr. Hubbard's honor; however, a town board meeting in 1859 ended with a decision to change the name to Osceola in reverence for the Seminole chief.

Mill companies flourished through the early 1900s, and Osceola Landing was the construction site of the St. Croix River's first steamboat, another epoch that

A peek at Osceola Falls

Osceola Falls' lower veil

thrived for roughly three decades until the railroad heralded an entirely new chapter of America's landscape. Indeed, Osceola's present-day identity is intricately tied to its rich history, and you can feel it on this short, lively hike.

From the Chief Osceola statue on Cascade Street, follow the long stairway down into a densely wooded glen harboring Osceola Creek. Without hesitation, hikers are treated to a stop-and-linger view of Cascade Falls, a surprisingly impressive waterfall plunging in a wide curtain from a ledge of the steep sandstone bluff. From here, a couple of wooden bridges parallel the creek's serenade along the base of the bluff, adjacent to a mini plantation of prolifically populating reedgrass.

A gentle curve leads past an idyllic creek-side home and under the highway bridge at the shore of the St. Croix River. A short spur trail leads to a sometimes-there view of the river, depending on season and leaf cover. Check it out and then start the long, switchback-y climb up to the top of Eagle Bluff. Hang a right on the Simenstad Trail, following the ridgeline to a pair of overlooks with splendiferous views of the river valley. The trail curves through the forest and heads back northeast. Pass the junction with Eagle Bluff Trail and continue to a tidy little picnic area near the highway. Cross the highway here to a bridge with a beauteous look at the creek's homestretch to the falls before wrapping up the hike.

Of great delight to me is the trailhead's proximity to two of Osceola's best out-door patios. Score a refreshing post-hike brew at PY's or treat the kids to ice cream at the Wisconsin Milkhouse. Good times!

Falls Bluff Loop–Osceola

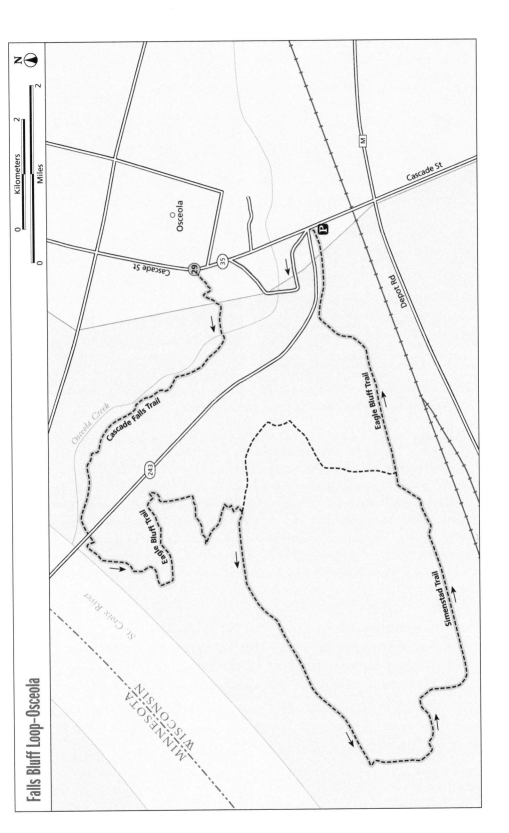

Osceola Creek (left); hiking a short boardwalk on the trail (right)

Why Go?

Just north of Osceola is Osceola Bedrock Glades, a large and very rare compilation of exposed bedrock, one of only four in Wisconsin. This site is packed with a robust glade environment of ferns, fungi, moss-covered logs, and lichen-stained rocks. Exposed bedrock is rare in its own right, and with an unreliable water source and nearly barren of soil, only the hardiest, specially adapted flora can survive, such as ground-level grasses and herbs and patchy woodlands of stunted trees. The Osceola glade site also boasts a healthy population of prairie fame-flower, a Wisconsin Special Concern plant.

Miles and Directions

0.0   Follow Cascade Falls Trail past Cascade Falls and along the creek.

0.3   Pass under the highway bridge. Check out the spur trail for more river views.

0.5   Reach junction with the Simenstad Trail; turn right and follow this path along the ridge.

0.9   Pass the trail from Eagle Bluff. Continue across the highway to the bridge over the creek.

1.2   Arrive back at the trailhead.

30 Sandrock Cliffs

Stand atop 500-million-year-old cliffs on this short, family-friendly hike on Wisconsin's western border, with easy access camping for an optional overnighter.

Distance: 3 miles, with options for more
Difficulty: Easy
Photogenic factor: 4
Hiking time: 90 minutes
Trail surface: Hard-packed dirt with grassy sections
Other trail users: None
Canine compatibility: Leashed pets allowed

Land status: National park service
Fees and permits: None
Maps: Park service maps; USGS Bass Creek MN
Trail contacts: St. Croix National Riverway, 401 Hamilton St., St. Croix Falls, WI 54024; (715) 483-2274; nps.gov/sacn

Finding the trailhead: From Grantsburg, follow Highway 70 west 4.6 miles to the St. Croix River boat landing on the left. The trailhead is at the far northwest end. **Trailhead GPS:** N45 77.477' / W92 92.779'

The Hike

This relaxing day hike follows a section of linked loops in dense, second-growth hardwood forest along the renowned St. Croix River. Flowing roughly 170 miles from its headwaters at Wisconsin's Upper St. Croix Lake, the river's lively flow and accompanying northwoods scenery was granted federal designation as a wild and scenic river in 1968, protecting critical habitat for waterfowl, including wood ducks, mallards, blue-winged teal, herons, and many duck species. Below the surface, walleye, northern, bass, and muskie thrive, while inland from the river's banks, white-tailed deer roam the woods, along with robust populations of beaver, black bear, muskrat, ruffed grouse, and fox. A paddler's delight, the upper St. Croix still retains its wilderness pedigree, with only hints of human encroachment, while steep limestone cliffs and deep valleys highlight the landscape farther south.

Not surprisingly, the St. Croix has provided home, sustenance, and transportation for people for thousands of years. Dakota, Ojibwe, and many other American Indian tribes already occupied the area when European settlers arrived in the 1600s, introducing a thriving fur trade and soon after, the logging boom that wiped out vast pine forests across Minnesota and Wisconsin. The sandstone cliffs we see today were born 500 million years ago when an enormous, shallow sea slowly evaporated and left behind deposits of sand that compressed into rock. Glacial events then did their thing, scraping and gouging and eventually draining ancient Lake Duluth, which roared south in eons-long construction, forming what we see today.

A calm stretch of the St. Croix

This short loop at riverside is a splendid day out in peaceful woods, with aromatic pine stands, linger-worthy river views, quiet campsites on the north end of the loop, and of course the high cliffs. It also gets bonus points for the paddle-access campsite that makes an unforgettable getaway. Start the hike at the boat landing on Highway 70 and walk a narrow dirt path through stands of white and red pine that rapidly give way to a hardwood mix of maple, birch, ash, and scattered aspen. A couple of short spur trails lead to river overlooks and soon the trail enters another pine neighborhood with spongy tread below your feet and wind whispers overhead. Follow a gradual climb to the tops of the cliffs, where well-trod social trails trace a contour high above the river. It's hard to resist getting close to the edge for the best views but use your noggin, steer clear, and hold tight to young hikers; sandstone crumbles easily and it's a long way down.

The designated trail meets another path heading north, as well as a handful of campsites, and then turns back for the southbound return. This stretch passes through an all-hardwood forest, with only occasional appearances of pines. You'll see intermittent glimpses of a lake and gravel pit to the east and soon the path gradually descends to the lower pine stands and back to the trailhead.

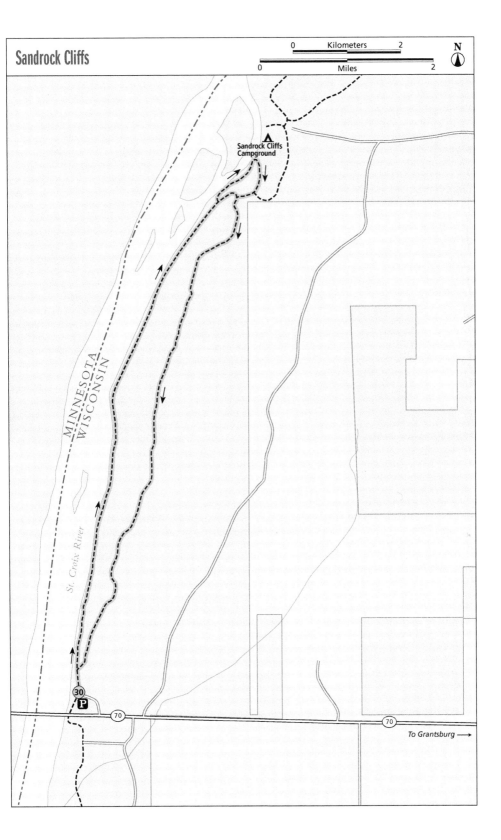

Kilometers

0 2

0 Miles 2

N

Sandrock Cliffs
Campground

MINNESOTA
WISCONSIN

St. Croix River

30
P

70

70

To Grantsburg →

Needle-covered trail along the river (left); the St. Croix from the cliffs (right)

Why Go?

The St. Croix National Scenic Riverway is one of America's original eight National Wild and Scenic Rivers, a designation that protects the more than 250 miles of clear, cold, fish-filled waters of the St. Croix and Namekagon Rivers. Managed by the National Park Service and partner agencies, staff and volunteers work to promote forest stewardship, habitat restoration, land protection, and invasive species management. Educational programs like Wild River Conservancy's Rivers are Alive offer hands-on teaching that connects students to this priceless liquid landscape.

Miles and Directions

0.0 Hike north from the trailhead, paralleling the river. A pair of spur trails lead to the water's edge.

1.2 Arrive at the cliffs area. Circle back south through the campsites, staying right at the junction with a trail leading east, to complete the loop on the main trail.

3.0 Arrive back at the trailhead.

31 Willow River State Park

This wildly popular state park is packed with variety from open prairie to river gorges, all steeped in pioneer history.

Distance: 3.4 miles, with options for additional miles
Difficulty: Easy with 1 moderate grade
Photogenic factor: 4
Hiking time: About 90 minutes
Trail surface: Hard-packed dirt with scattered rocks
Other trail users: None

Canine compatibility: Leashed pets allowed
Land status: State park
Fees and permits: Vehicle pass required
Maps: State park maps; USGS Stillwater, MN
Trail contacts: Willow River State Park, 1034 County Highway A, Hudson, WI 54016; (715) 386-5931; dnr.wi.gov/topic/parks/name/willowriver

Finding the trailhead: From I-94, exit at US 12 and head north 1.6 miles to CR U. Keep going north on CR U for 0.3 mile to its junction with CR A. Follow CR A north 1.5 miles to the park entrance. **Trailhead GPS:** N45 01.736' / W92 67.437'

The Hike

Nearly within shouting distance of Hudson, Willow River State Park is a 3,000-acre playground of prairie, forest, and scenic riverway. The park's namesake river flows in at its northeastern corner, ambles a bit, and roars through a 200-foot gorge before slowing to a crawl at Little Falls Lake, which doubles as a marshy area depending on water flow. From here, the river winds about 3 more as-the-crow-flies miles to its confluence with the St. Croix.

As was all the rage in the late 1800s, logging grandly exploited this area, and the Willow River served as a handy transportation corridor to shuttle felled timber to Hudson and lumber mills downstream on the St. Croix. Early settlers also harnessed the river's energy to run power plants that supplied electricity to Hudson. Two of the three dams inserted into the river for this purpose have been removed so far, and the area is still in stages of active restoration. Look for evidence of young prairie grasses and wildflowers, plentiful terrestrial wildlife, and all manner of birds, amphibians, and waterfowl.

Prior to logging and settler days, the area's rice lakes were highly coveted by American Indian tribes, and 1785's great Battle of Willow River saw the Chippewa and Sioux fighting it out to claim the coveted lakes.

Today this is one of Wisconsin's most visited state parks, with 13 miles of trails, three separate campgrounds, nature center, and, of course, the falls. Rock climbers also flock to the park to take on 5.1 to 5.9 routes on designated walls of the gorge. Winter serves up fun in fifty shades of white, with sledding, snowshoeing, and winter camping.

Heading toward Willow Falls KENT MERHAR

This short hike samples a couple of the park's scenic and historic sections, with close-up views of Willow Falls and its neighboring lake. Head down the hill from the trailhead to the river gorge and take a short side trip to see the falls. A stairway leads the way along a 100-foot drop in elevation to a close-up view of the lively waterfall. Back on the main route, the heavily wooded trail of maple, aspen, scattered oak, ash, and other species hugs the shoreline of Little Falls Lake, which for much of the year is more of a marsh than a lake. Experts call this an impoundment drawdown; a fancy term for the presence of a dam and associated fluctuations in water level.

From the lake, the trail heads straight for the north side of the 300 Campground. Simply follow the road to the left to meet up with the Pioneer Trail. This path squiggles past two more campgrounds and historical grave sites of the area's first white settlers on its way back to the trailhead.

Why Go?

Just east of the state park is Willow River Wildlife Area, 800 acres of restored prairie and now-rare oak savanna. Plantation of red and white pine host an array of wildlife and the property is part of the Western Prairie Habitat Restoration Area, an extensive effort to restore and protect 20,000 acres of critical grasslands and wetlands with a primary focus on biodiversity and habitat establishment for native birds and waterfowl.

Willow River State Park

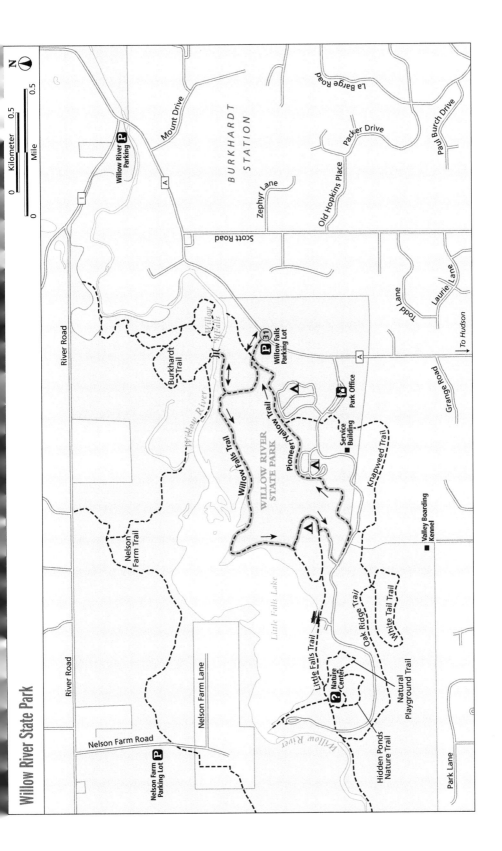

A quiet place along the river KENT MERHAR

Miles and Directions

0.0 From the Willow Falls parking area, hike past the Pioneer Trail and head down a moderately steep stairway toward Willow Falls.

0.4 At the trail fork, go right to check out the falls, then continue on the main loop on Willow Falls Trail heading west past Little Falls Lake.

2.0 Arrive at the 300 Campground. Turn left and follow the circle road to connect to the Pioneer Trail. Follow the Pioneer Trail past the 200 Campground and back to the trailhead.

3.4 Arrive back at the trailhead.

32 Hoffman Hills Recreation Area

Hoffman boasts 9 miles of trails laced throughout 700 acres of blissfully quiet forest, prairie, and wetlands with bonus points for 360-degree views of it all from a 60-foot observation tower.

Distance: 2.7 miles, with options for additional miles
Difficulty: Challenging
Photogenic factor: 5
Hiking time: 45–60 minutes
Trail surface: Wide grassy trail and packed dirt
Other trail users: None
Canine compatibility: Leashed pets allowed

Land status: State recreation area
Fees and permits: Vehicle pass required
Maps: DNR map; USGS Rusk
Trail contacts: Wisconsin DNR, 101 South Webster St., Madison, WI 53707; (888) 936-7463 or Hoffman Hills Recreation Area at (715) 232-1242; dnr.wisconsin.gov/topic/parks/hoffmanhills

Finding the trailhead: From the I-94/CR B exit northeast of Menomonie: head north on CR B for 2.6 miles and then turn east on 730th Avenue. Continue east for 2 miles and turn south on 690th Street. Turn east again after 0.2 mile on 720th Avenue and follow for 1.4 miles to the park entrance at the junction with 740th Street. **Trailhead GPS:** N44 56.392' / W91 46.578'

The Hike

In 1980, Richard and Marian Hoffman donated 280 acres of their rural farmland to the Wisconsin Department of Natural Resources, an enormously generous gift that has since become one of the state's most treasured outdoor retreats. Situated in the Western Coulee and Ridges Region, Hoffman Hills boasts more than 700 acres of densely wooded terrain scrunched like a messy blanket; wetlands packed with frogs, turtles, ducks, and other waterfowl; and an expansive tallgrass prairie. A 9-mile trail system snakes throughout the hills, much to the joy of area outdoors lovers who fancy hiking, cross-country skiing, sledding, or bird watching. Hidden in plain sight not far from Menomonie, the area is pleasantly uncrowded aside from a vibrant wildlife population. You are likely to hear woodpeckers perforating trees nearby, bluebird accents in the prairie and raptors above it, plenty of white-tailed deer, and dozens of songbird species.

The trails are cut wide to accommodate classic and skate skiers, and diligently maintained year-round for hikers as well. The tough part (or perhaps the best part) is choosing which trail to take, what with the diversity in scenery. I tend to gravitate toward the woods and Hoffman serves it up in extra-large helpings, mixing flavors of aromatic white and red pine with resplendent hardwood species such as birch, maple, ash, oak, and lots more. Every trail junction is marked with maps affixed to signposts, so getting lost will happen only if approached intentionally. The observation tower is

A farmstead at the base of the hill

naturally a big draw and its allure pulled me to it like a magnet. I can't resist the challenge of big hills, and views from up high are always grand.

The trail starts with a respectable uphill grind on the Plantation Trail over a wide ridge and down the other side to the Lower Pines Trail. Turn right and hike to the Upper Pines Trail into its namesake trees on a rolling track with an elevation track resembling an earthquake seismic graph. Expect to hike up and down a lot in these hills but it is oh, so worth it.

Merge onto the Logging Road and curve up Hawk Ridge Trail to the observation tower. Several platforms are built in from bottom to top, each with great views, but the highest of course delivers extraordinary panoramas of bucolic Wisconsin countryside. Menomonie is also visible to the southwest. The tower's high perch is the perfect place for mid-hike lunch break or rest stop.

After the views, descend from the tower and hike past an aspen stand above a deep valley to a steep drop on the Roller Coaster Trail and the Logging Road junction. This time, turn right and cruise along a relatively flat section to Lower Pines. Keep descending, veering left at all junctions back to the Plantation Trail and the return to the trailhead.

Highly recommended for more miles or your next trip: Hike across the road from the trailhead to the Catherine Hoffman-Hartl Memorial Wetland Trail and onward to the double loop around Marion's and Richard's Ponds. The savannah loops north of the ponds are also ideal for spotting lively and melodic birds and other ground-based critters.

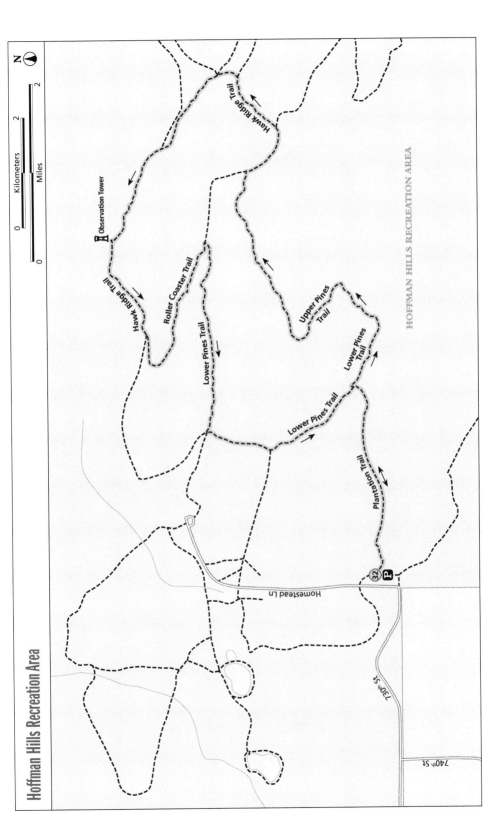

Hoffman Hills Recreation Area

Observation Tower

Hawk Ridge Trail

Roller Coaster Trail

Hawk Ridge Trail

Lower Pines Trail

Upper Pines Trail

Lower Pines Trail

Lower Pines Trail

Plantation Trail

Homestead Ln

730th St

740th St

32

HOFFMAN HILLS RECREATION AREA

N

Kilometers
0   2

Miles
0   2

Morning light on the trail

Curving through the pines (left); feathertopped trail marker (right)

Why Go?

Large-scale, contiguous landscapes are rare all over the country, and Wisconsin is no exception. Hoffman Hills provides the canvas as well as the built-in bonus of several distinct ecosystems: hardwood forest, pine forest, wetland, and prairie. This serves as ideal study and management areas to promote conservation and preservation of wildlife habitat, forest restoration, and protection of rare and threatened flora.

Miles and Directions

0.0 Hike east on the Plantation Trail.

0.3 Turn right on Lower Pines and left on Upper Pines near the group camp area.

0.8 Merge right onto Logging Road.

1.1 Merge onto Hawk Ridge Trail.

1.4 Arrive at the observation tower and climb up for great views.

1.6 After leaving the tower, reach junction with Roller Coaster Trail and turn left.

1.8 Turn right on Logging Road and veer left at the next two junctions.

2.4 Right turn on Plantation Trail.

2.7 Arrive back at the trailhead.

33 Chippewa Moraine State Recreation Area—Circle Trail

Moraines and swales, knobs and kettles. See it all on this breathlessly scenic hike that winds through gently rolling forest littered with glacial lakes.

Distance: 4.5 miles, with options for additional miles
Difficulty: Easy
Photogenic factor: 4+
Hiking time: About 2 hours
Trail surface: Hard-packed dirt path with scattered rocks
Other trail users: None

Canine compatibility: Leashed pets allowed
Land status: State land
Fees and permits: None
Maps: Ice Age Trail maps; USGS Bloomer
Trail contacts: Chippewa Moraine State Recreation Area, 1339 CR M, New Auburn, WI 54757; (715) 967-2800; dnr.wi.gov/topic/parks/name/chipmoraine

Finding the trailhead: From Main Street in New Auburn, follow CR SS north to CR M and turn right. Go east on CR M 8 miles to the Chippewa Moraine State Recreation Area entrance road. The trailhead is next to the visitor center. **Trailhead GPS:** N45 13.430' / W91 24.826'

The Hike

Along with drop-dead gorgeous scenery, the Chippewa Moraine area is packed with options. Do a short out-and-back hike to the lakes, make a big loop on the Circle Trail, kick back in a wide-open meadow, or throw on a pack and hit the Ice Age Trail for a multiday adventure. This part of Wisconsin is perforated with dozens of glacially bred lakes tucked in the folds of gently rolling topography and resplendent forests. Distractingly scenic, to be sure, and a great place to connect with your wild side. This is officially called a southern dry mesic forest, and it's packed with colorful and melodious songbirds, such as scarlet tanagers, cardinals, woodpeckers, and yellow-throated vireos. On the ground you're likely to see white-tailed deer all over the place, and don't be surprised to hear a loud slap on the water from resident beavers.

The Chippewa Moraine region you are walking in today is part of Wisconsin's Ice Age National Scientific Reserve, a group of nine units across the state set aside to protect glacial landscapes with special scientific and scenic value. Established in 1964 as a program of the National Park System, the reserve is loaded with incredible displays of our glacial past for study, outdoor recreation, camping, and birding. Want to learn more? The Chippewa Moraine Chapter of the Ice Age Trail Alliance is your go-to source for all kinds of great events, such as the Parade of Colors hike, and volunteering with trail crews. Find all kinds of great info at iceagetrail.org. Plan some time before or after this hike to check out the well-appointed visitor center, chock-full of fascinating, glacier-inspired information.

Bridge crossing on the trail

Secluded lake along the trail

From the trailhead perched just north of the visitor center, head east into the woods on the Ice Age/Circle Trail. The skinny path descends for a short while and makes a gentle curve to the northeast past a few Ice Age–bred kettle lakes. A trailside bench is a perfect spot to stop and enjoy the outrageous beauty of these woods. From here, cross a wooden bridge and follow the path on a wide hairpin into resplendent forest and a couple more pothole lakes to CR M.

Cross the road and climb gradually up a moraine, hiking south between a pair of hidden lakes to a junction with the Ice Age Trail, which heads off far eastbound.

HILLTOP LAKES

The sculpting work of glaciers isn't always about deep gorges and dramatic valleys. In the Wisconsin Glaciation period, depressions in glaciers collected water to form small lakes that were then surrounded by extra-large ice blocks. Assorted debris collected on lake bottoms, and when the ice blocks melted, the debris stayed behind as fine sediment and formed the flat-topped hills we see today. Scoops from the ground attracted meltwater, which in turn created kettle lakes.

Chippewa Moraine State Recreation Trail–
Ice Age Trail

NORTH OF NORTH SHATTUCK LAKE STATE NATURAL AREA

North of North Shattuck Lake

Payne Lake

Ace-in-the-Hole Lake

Horseshoe Lake

Ice Age/Circle Trail

North Shattuck Lake

33

❓ 🅿️
Chippewa Moraine
Ice Age Unit
Interpretive Center

Rudolph Road

Irving Road

Weeks Lakes

M

Jeanstow Lake

258th Avenue

S Shattuck Road

South Shattuck Lake

Ebbens Road

Chippewa County

M

Beauteous woods and rolling, wooded hills ensue on the way past South Shattuck Lake. The trail curves north, following the crest of a glacial esker, and crosses CR M again. Enjoy views of no less than five more lakes, including North Shattuck and North of North Shattuck, where a welcoming bench awaits in the shadow of a stand of white pines. Cross a wooden bridge and climb the final stretch to the trailhead.

Why Go?

This area of Wisconsin contains some of our country's most dramatic visual evidence of Earth's glacial past. What we see today is the result of a wall of ice 2 miles thick that chugged south from Canada and came to a stop about a mile south of this hike's trailhead. Untold tons of sand, rocks, and other debris were pushed into the stalled ice sheet and scattered about when the ice melted.

Lake views from the trailhead

Wooden bridge crossing

Miles and Directions

0.0 Hike east from the trailhead, passing a handful of kettle lakes and trailside bench. Veer right at the junction with the Circle Trail.

0.9 Cross CR M.

1.5 Stay right at the Ice Age Trail junction.

3.5 Cross CR M again and follow the trail north and east past more lakes and another trailside bench to the Interpretive Center.

4.5 Arrive back at the trailhead.

34 Timms Hill

It's not high enough to officially be called a mountain and altitude sickness isn't a worry, but a hike up Timms Hill gets you 40-mile views and a notch in your state high point belt.

Distance: 1.2 miles
Difficulty: Easy
Photogenic factor: 4
Hiking time: 45 minutes
Trail surface: Dirt and grass mix
Other trail users: None
Canine compatibility: Leashed pets allowed

Land status: County park
Fees and permits: None
Maps: Park map; USGS Timms Hill
Trail contacts: Price County Parks, 104 South Eyder Ave., Phillips, WI 54555; (715) 339-6371; co.price.wi.us

Finding the trailhead: From Ogema, follow WI 86 4 miles east to CR C and turn left. Follow CR C 1.2 miles to the park entrance. The trailhead parking area is 0.6 mile on the left. **Trailhead GPS:** N45 27.012' / W90 11.327'

The Hike

For a long time, Rib Mountain was hailed as Wisconsin's highest point, and it certainly looks more impressive than Timms. Rib's summit stands nearly 700 feet above the surrounding terrain, lending a more mountain-y look, but you can't argue with elevation and at 1,951.5 feet, Timms Hill gets the nod. The official geographical threshold for a hill to claim status as a "mountain" is 2,000 feet (Timms misses by 48.5 feet) and it ranks thirty-ninth out of the country's 50 state high points—not exactly a Rocky Mountain high—but in Wisconsin this is still revered terrain, the state's highest natural point and among the highest in the Upper Midwest.

At the top of the hill, a wooden observation tower offers an additional elevation boost above the trees for 360 degrees of some of our state's best views, especially spectacular in the fall when it feels as if you're looking down on an ocean of smoldering embers. Timms Lake and Bass Lake are also in view from way up there. A state high point survey marker is stuck in the ground below the tower, marking the hill's formal

CONCRETE CREATIONS

Fred Smith always had a use for leftover concrete. A retired lumberjack, Smith started creating sculptures made of concrete, glass bottles, and other random objects. He amassed quite a collection of weighty artwork, at one time numbering more than 200, many of which still stand on Smith's property in Phillips.

Faraway views from the tower GOODFREEPHOTOS.COM

dedication. Blanketing the hill and spread out in all directions is a vibrant forest blend of various northern pine species and hardwoods, including basswood, birch, ash, and ubiquitous sugar maple, the latter providing ample ingredients for thriving maple syrup enterprises hereabouts. Here's a fun trivia nugget: Timms is almost exactly half-way between the equator and the North Pole.

My favorite part of Timms Hill is it's not close to any big, bustling tourist towns; it's out in the veritable middle of nowhere, and that makes it the perfect getaway. The county park surrounding the hill used to be an old logging camp, owned by Timothy Gahan, and the hill was named for its former owner. Price County purchased the camp and created the park in 1983.

Tracking south of the park is the 10-mile Timms Hill Trail, a connector trail built in 1986 by members of two area cross-country ski clubs. The path links the hill to the 1,200-mile-long Ice Age Trail and in addition to a hiker favorite, this is a popular go-to for skiers and snowshoers. It is also America's first federally designated side trail in the National Trails System.

From the trailhead, follow the well-traveled dirt path through the woods on a steady grade to the observation tower. Scramble up there for a look around and then retreat to the trail and turn left to start a counterclockwise loop around the base of the hill. The trail parallels the southern shoreline of Timms Lake and a bench about

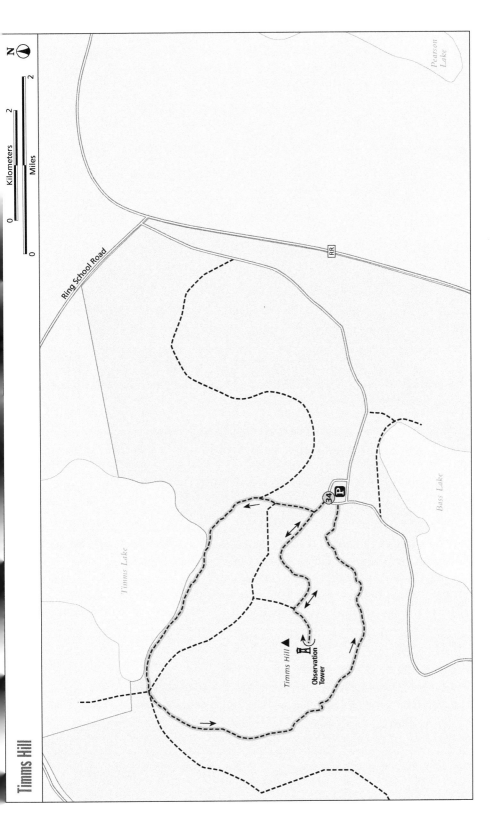

Skinny trail on the way to the tower DENICE BREAUX

halfway along offers a comfy place to take in lakeside views. From here, the path alternates between dirt and grass tread, with a brief glimpse of Bass Lake on the homestretch to the trailhead. This is a great little hike in one of our state's best locales. Don't miss the Hill of Beans Café at the south end of Bass Lake for post-hike refreshments.

Why Go?

It's no secret that old forests are a rare sight in Wisconsin, but the North Central Forest region offers ideal conditions for effective regeneration, particularly in maintaining large habitat and establishing connection of patchy or missing forest habitat. Of specific interest to forest officials is regeneration of hemlock and yellow birch to a point of a managed old-growth environment.

Miles and Directions

0.0 Hike up the hill to the observation tower.

0.2 Reach the tower, climb it, and enjoy the views before returning to the trail.

0.4 Turn left and hike toward Timms Lake. Score lakeside views at the trailside bench.

1.2 Arrive back at the trailhead.

35 Kinnickinnic State Park

The Kinnickinnic River, known as the Kinni, is revered by Wisconsinites for its outstanding fishing and solitude. This leisurely hike wanders through some of the park's scenic standouts, with a side trip down the bluff to the St. Croix River.

Distance: 2.6 miles, with option for additional miles
Difficulty: Easy with 1 steep section to the river
Photogenic factor: 4+
Hiking time: About 1 hour
Trail surface: Hard-packed dirt and gravel and short paved section
Other trail users: None

Canine compatibility: Leashed pets allowed
Land status: State park
Fees and permits: Vehicle pass required
Maps: State park maps; USGS Prescott
Trail contacts: Kinnickinnic State Park, W11983 820th Ave., River Falls, WI 54022; (715) 425-1129; dnr.wi.gov/topic/parks/name/kinnickinnic

Finding the trailhead: From I-94 in Hudson, exit at CR F and head south 9 miles to 820th Avenue. Turn right and the park entrance is 0.2 mile on the left. Follow the park road 1.2 miles to the picnic and trail parking area on the left. **Trailhead GPS:** N44 83.401' / W92 75.139'

The Hike

It looks like a tranquil, meandering stream, and while it is indeed a beauty, the Kinni is a Department of Natural Resources–designated Outstanding Resource Water and nationally recognized Class I trout stream boasting stretches of more than 8,000 trout per mile. This gorgeous, spring-fed river runs 22 miles through idyllic western Wisconsin countryside, with a 174-square-mile (96,000-acre) watershed that includes 40 percent of the state's plant species, 50 percent of bird species, and nearly fifty types of critters on the endangered, threatened, or special concern list.

The Lower Kinni, below the River Falls dams, is a twisting, raggedy canyon millions of years old, escaping the cold hand of ancient glaciers. The canyon proper starts a mile or so west of River Falls and runs all the way to the St. Croix. High, sheer cliffs are the main feature, clad in moss and ferns with scattered rapids below. Wildlife in many forms make homes or regularly visit the canyon, including high-flying eagles, great blue herons, waterfowl galore, and white-tailed deer all over the place. A particularly spectacular accoutrement in the canyon are the Weeping Cliffs, named for

ANCIENT ORIGINS

Fun-to-say Kinnickinnic (originally spelled with a k at the end) is an early American Indian smoking mixture made from a combination of plant leaves and various barks. In fact, the Ojibwe meaning is literally "things that are mixed."

Spectacular fall colors along the St. Croix River KENT MERHAR

underground aquifers that seep through the limestone walls. The steady water supply and a cool, shady environment on the canyon's north side is an incubator of vibrant green mosses and ferns, as well as white pine (rare in this part of the state). The southern flanks host steeply sloped "goat prairies." We're proud to call the Kinni our own.

This short hike starts in the heart of the park on the Orange Trail, skirting the edge of a prairie for a few dozen steps before heading into dense woods of largely mixed hardwood, with red and white pine scattered about. A half mile later the path meets the Purple Trail. Follow this trail as it curves along the top of the river gorge, with intermittent views to the river below.

When the trail reaches the picnic area at the far western end of the park, linger for a bit at the overlook above the Kinnickinnic Delta far below, then take the short, steep paved path down to the swimming beach and outrageous upstream views of the St. Croix River. The Kinni empties into the St. Croix through the trees just south of here, and on sunny summer weekends, the St. Croix bustles with water-based activity when vessels of all shapes and sizes take to the water like ants to a picnic basket. Even if you don't have one, it's fun to kick back and watch all the boats float up and down the river.

After a break, head back uphill to the Purple Trail and follow it east (right). In short order you'll meet the Yellow Trail, turn left, passing an optional 1-mile loop on the Green Trail. The main loop crosses the park road and leads right back to the parking area and trailhead.

Insider's tip: Don't miss plunging down the sledding hill in winter and snowshoeing through the woods along the gorge.

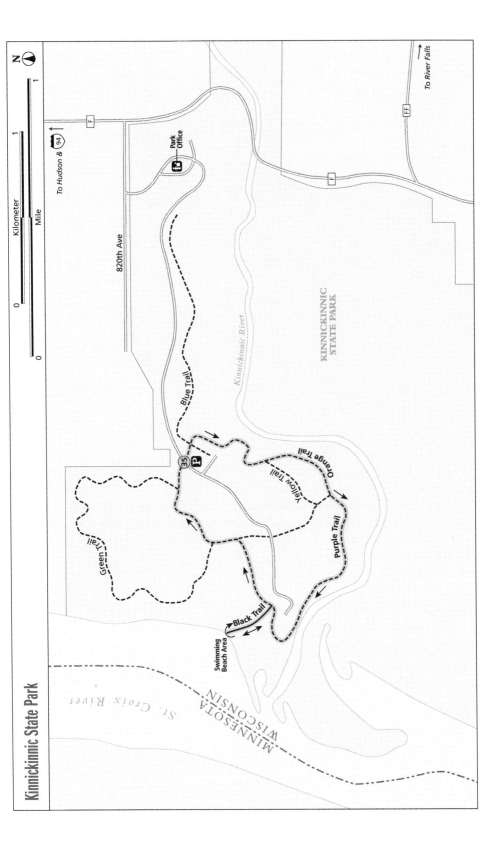

Kinnickinnic State Park

Wide, woodsy trail KENT MERHAR

Why Go?

The Upper Kinni watershed is known for its slower, colder water coveted by brown trout. In fact, 8,000 browns per mile have been recorded on this stretch, well beyond the Department of Natural Resource's highest rating. Thanks to an array of tributary creeks, this part of the river remains vibrant with underwater life. Dedicated efforts from groups such as the Kinnickinnic River Land Trust (KRLT) help ensure it stays that way. Recent work by KRLT is focused on the purchase of a 40-acre old-growth forest parcel in the lower canyon.

Miles and Directions

0.0   Set off from the trailhead on the Orange Trail, past the prairie and into the trees.

0.4   Reach junction with the Purple Trail, turn left.

1.1   Arrive at the picnic area and overlook. Head 600 feet downhill to the river and back up to continue on the Purple Trail.

1.6   Reach junction with the Yellow Trail, turn left. Pass (or take) the Green Trail option.

2.6   Arrive back at the trailhead.

36 Perrot State Park

This lumpy park in Wisconsin's southwest is home to the confluence of the Trempealeau and Mississippi Rivers and sublime views of the valley from Perrot Ridge or Brady's Bluff.

Distance: 3.1 miles
Difficulty: Moderate with 2 steep climbs (many other trail options available)
Photogenic factor: 4+
Hiking time: 2+ hours
Trail surface: Hard-packed dirt with scattered roots and rocks, and a section of stairs
Other trail users: None

Canine compatibility: Leashed pets allowed
Land status: State park
Fees and permits: Vehicle pass required
Maps: State park maps; USGS Winona, MN
Trail contacts: Perrot State Park, W26247 Sullivan Rd., Trempealeau, WI 54661; (608) 534-6409; dnr.wi.gov/topic/parks/name/perrot

Finding the trailhead: From La Crosse, follow US 53/WI 35 north 9.7 miles to the WI 35 exit. Head west 7.7 miles to Main Street in Trempealeau. Turn left and go 3 blocks to 1st Street. Turn right and follow 1st Street (which becomes South Park Road) 1.9 miles to the park entrance. **Trailhead GPS:** N44 01.626' / W91 47.542'

The Hike

Think back 500 million years or so to when an enormous inland sea covered today's Wisconsin. All that water drained as the land rose, and later another sea moved in. The advance and retreat of these inland seas piled up lots of mud and debris, creating the dramatic sandstone bluffs of today's Perrot State Park. Many of these steep, lumpy bluffs rise to more than 500 feet above verdant wetlands, open fields, and deep valleys, providing homes to hundreds of species of flora and fauna.

Indeed, Perrot is a veritable who's who of the upper Midwest nature scene, including water-loving critters such as beavers, mink, waterfowl, various turtles, all sorts of frogs and toads, and muskrats. Dense forests harbor plentiful white-tailed deer, foxes, woodchucks, and lots of squirrels. But perhaps the park's most popular wildlife highlight is found overhead. Well over 200 species of birds live in or migrate through this area every year, including warblers, flycatchers, vireos, and untold numbers of eagles and hawks. You might even catch a glimpse of tundra swans in the spring.

As if that wasn't enough, the park includes two Wisconsin State Natural Areas: Brady's Bluff Prairie and Trempealeau Mountain. Brady's is a dolomite-capped bluff bursting with native Wisconsin plants such as needle grass, prairie larkspur, and silky aster. Several rare butterfly species live here too. Across the Trempealeau River stands its namesake mountain at 425 feet and covered in oak, basswood, and maple. A long time ago the mountain served as a handy navigational reference for river travelers and

The Mississippi River valley from Perrot Ridge KENT MERHAR

merchants. Today it hosts many American Indian burial sites and other evidence of the area's rich history. Hikers can score stellar views of this hill from the top of Brady's.

About a dozen steps from the West Brady's Trailhead, the ground points upward in a hurry. Keep chugging along. Near the last pitch before the summit of Brady's Bluff, a very long set of stairs clings to the rocks to aid your final, heroic push. Okay, so it's not as dramatic as Everest and a tad lower in elevation, but the views from the top take your breath away all the same. Trempealeau Mountain is front and center in the foreground to the north, along with ridiculously gorgeous views of bluffs on the

WISCONSIN'S DRIFTLESS AREA

The last glacier that slunk down slowly from present-day Canada is responsible for much of Wisconsin's varied landscapes—except for the southwestern corner. The conglomeration of silt, sand, boulders, and other assorted debris left in the wake of glaciers is called drift. The giant glacier skipped this part of the state, hence its Driftless Area name, leaving behind outrageously beautiful, forested bluffs; deep coulees; and bucolic valleys.

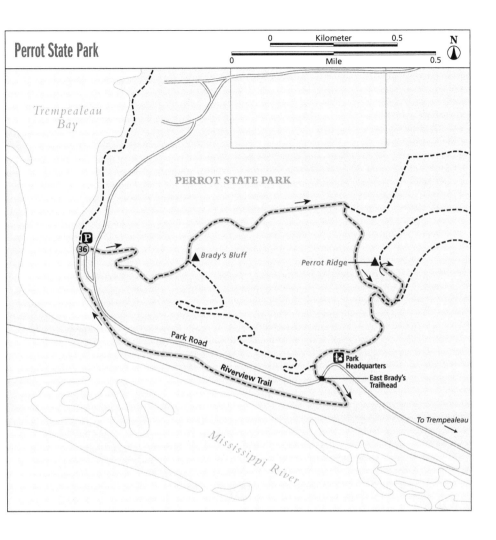

0   Kilometer   0.5   **N**

0   Mile   0.5

Trempealeau Bay

PERROT STATE PARK

P 36

▲ *Brady's Bluff*

Perrot Ridge ▲

Park Road

i Park Headquarters

Riverview Trail

East Brady's Trailhead

To Trempealeau

Mississippi River

Minnesota side and the long, winding upstream ribbon of the Mississippi. Views south are equally sublime. After soaking it all in, head northeast on Brady's Bluff Trail and drop down from the bluff into the shallow saddle between Brady's and Perrot Ridge.

By now you've likely noticed the colorful and lively display of resident woodland flowers in the form of Dutchman's breeches; phlox; violets in blue, yellow, and white; ferns; and bellwort. Especially in spring, the park is chock-full of aromatic plants dressed to the nines.

Turn right and follow the Deer Me Run Trail south, round the bulbous southern nose of the ridge, and hoof it up a short, steepish climb to the top for more life-list views. Descend and connect with the downhill East Brady's Trail to the park office and East Brady's Trailhead. Find the Riverview Trail at the edge of the parking area and wander this flat stretch along the railroad tracks and river back to the West Brady's Trailhead.

The Mississippi River KENT MERHAR

A long climb to the top KENT MERHAR

Trempealeau Mountain at sunset KENT MERHAR

Why Go?

Habitat loss and fragmentation are among the leading adversaries of wildlife's drive to survive and Perrot State Park is akin to an island of walnut, hickory and old-growth oak that support birds like the pileated woodpecker, scarlet tanager, and many of their brethren. A 2018 land donation to the Mississippi Valley Conservancy added 18 acres of ecologically significant land abutting the park that augments critical habitat of migratory songbirds along the Mississippi River.

Miles and Directions

0.0 From the West Brady's Trailhead, head into the woods, rapidly gaining elevation.

0.4 Reach the summit of Brady's Bluff and reach the junction with Brady's Bluff Trail. Turn left.

0.9 Reach the junction with Deer Me Run Trail, turn right.

1.3 Pass junction with the East Brady's Trail, but remember it; you'll return here for the descent. Continue to the next junction.

1.4 Turn left here for a short climb to the top of Perrot Ridge. Ogle the views and return to the junction you passed earlier.

1.9 Reach the East Brady's Trail and turn left for the descent to the East Brady's Trailhead.

2.2 Arrive at the East Brady's Trailhead. Head for the southeast corner of the parking lot and follow the sign for the Riverview Trail to meander back to the West Brady's Trailhead.

3.1 Arrive back at trailhead.

37 Wyalusing State Park

Score bluff-top views of two rivers, some of the state's best bird-watching, and explore the Treasure Cave on this long loop in Wisconsin's far southwest.

Distance: 4.1 miles
Difficulty: Moderate
Photogenic factor: 4+
Hiking time: 2+ hours
Trail surface: Hard-packed dirt path
Other trail users: None
Canine compatibility: Leashed pets allowed

Land status: State park
Fees and permits: Vehicle pass required
Maps: State park maps; USGS Brodtville, WI and USGS Clayton, IA
Trail contacts: Wyalusing State Park, 13081 State Park Ln., Bagley, WI 53801; (608) 996-2261; dnr.wi.gov/topic/parks/name/wyalusing

Finding the trailhead: From the junction of US 18 and WI 35 at the south end of Prairie du Chien, follow US 18 south 5 miles to CR C and turn right. Follow CR C south 3.1 miles to CR X and turn right. Go 1 mile west to the park entrance. Follow the park road 2 miles to the Green Cloud Picnic Area. The hike starts adjacent to the picnic shelter. **Trailhead GPS:** N42 98.869' / W91 12.869'

The Hike

In the nineteenth century, Munsee-Delaware American Indian tribes settled in this area at the confluence of the Mississippi and Wisconsin Rivers. In their Lenape language, Wyalusing means "home of the warrior." One can imagine proud tribes defending this special place of 500-foot-high bluffs and dense forests above the rivers. Indeed, effigy-shaped burial mounds dating back 3,000 years are evidence this area was held sacred for generations.

Today, Wyalusing State Park is 2,700 acres of dramatic bluff-top views, caves and fissures, and fantastical rock formations, along with wetlands, a canoe trail, river backwaters, and waterfalls. In the midst of it all is a long list of celebrity wildlife from the

SENTINEL RIDGE

At Wyalusing State Park's western boundary, Sentinel Ridge rises high above the Mississippi River Valley. On this ridge, 69 of more than 130 American Indian burial mounds are carefully preserved. Many original mounds were destroyed by rampant stone quarrying or farming, but we are fortunate today to share this space with the remaining mounds. The Sentinel Hill and Procession mound groups are made of twenty-eight mounds in linear formation following the crest of the bluff. Archaeologists and historians believe at least two separate periods of mound building were present in this area, with evidence including stone crypts, copper celt, and stone pipe.

Peaceful forest trail DENICE BREAUX

A leafy path parkway DENICE BREAUX

water to high overhead. Be on the lookout for beavers, foxes, deer, bald eagles, turkey vultures, and several raptor species.

Nearly one hundred bird species live here, with many more migrating through in spring and fall. You see and hear colorful songbirds, great horned owls, and woodpeckers. At ground level, look for wild turkey, white-tailed deer, snakes, squirrels, and lots more. The wetlands and river are home to all manner of waterfowl such as wood ducks, herons, and egrets, as well as muskrats, minks, and beavers.

This revered state park, originally named Nelson Dewey, is more than 100 years old, and its present form hosts two popular campgrounds, naturalist programs, and many other activities, such as bicycling, fishing and hunting, and cross-country skiing in winter. The park also holds national status through the Wyalusing Hardwood Forest, a National Natural Landmark, and the Wyalusing State Park Mounds Archeological District. Throw in the Wyalusing Hardwood Forest State Natural Area and you've got yourself a packed lineup of nature's best stuff.

Highlights for hikers are sprawling panoramic views, of which there are many, and you get a couple dandies on this gem of a hike. Start out on the Sentinel Ridge Trail and head north from the Green Cloud Picnic Area to the junction of the Old Immigrant Trail, which descends the bluff via a few switchbacks to the river. Take advantage of the bench that awaits and enjoy a relaxing mid-hike break. From here, the path makes a sweeping curve through the woods on its climb back up the bluff and the junction with the Bluff Trail. Follow this trail and don't miss the short side trip to the Knob for outrageous views of the Wisconsin River.

Wyalusing State Park

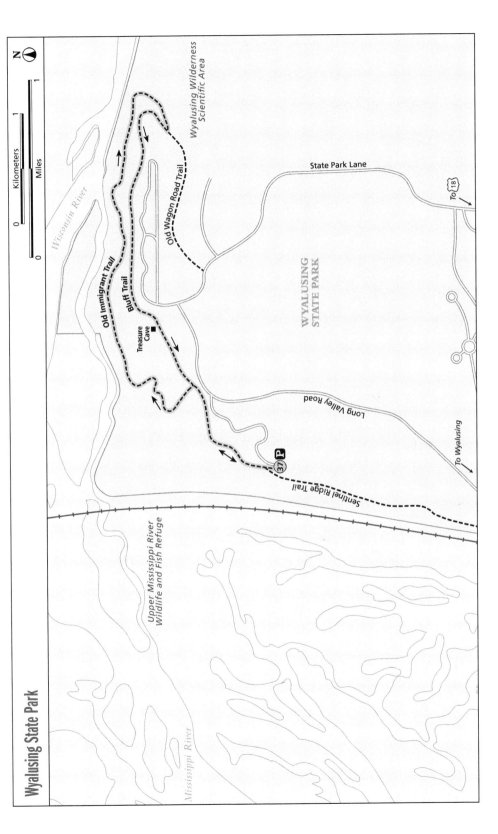

N

Kilometers
0   1

Miles
0   1

Wisconsin River

Wyalusing Wilderness Scientific Area

State Park Lane

To 18

Old Wagon Road Trail

Old Immigrant Trail

Bluff Trail

Treasure Cave

WYALUSING STATE PARK

Long Valley Road

P
3

To Wyalusing

Sentinel Ridge Trail

Upper Mississippi River Wildlife and Fish Refuge

Mississippi River

A wise old oak along the trail DENICE BREAUX

Keep on truckin' on the Bluff Trail and soon arrive at the short trail to Treasure Cave, one of the park's go-to destinations. A steep staircase leads up to the cave, and inside, you can shinny along through a narrow passage to a hidden chamber. Very cool stuff. Back on the trail are a couple more stairways, a stone archway, and another pair of overlooks.

Back at the Old Immigrant junction, turn right and follow the Sentinel Ridge Trail back to the trailhead.

Why Go?

Wyalusing Hardwood Forest State Natural Area includes a riveting display of vegetation continuum, a concept inspired by the late Dr. John Curtis, a University of Wisconsin botany professor. This area, within its namesake state park, is home to four southern forest types: wet-mesic, mesic, dry-mesic, and dry. Such diverse habitat naturally nurtures an incredibly rich animal population from the forest floor to river valley to skies overhead.

Miles and Directions

0.0 From the trailhead, hike north on the Sentinel Ridge Trail.

0.3 Reach junction with the Old Immigrant Trail, turn left and descend to the river.

2.9 Reach junction with the Bluff Trail, turn right. Don't miss the short spur trails to the Knob and Treasure Cave.

3.8 Reach junction with the Sentinel Ridge Trail, rejoin and keep going straight ahead.

4.1 Arrive back at the trailhead.

Southern Reaches

In Wisconsin's far south, hikers are treated to a little bit of everything, from steep bluffs and postcard scenery at Devil's Lake State Park to off-the-grid forest to relaxing lakeside walks at the University of Wisconsin's Arboretum and adjacent reserve. Whatever your fancy, you'll find it here, and your hiking boots will thank you.

Looking for insider tips from the author? Put Gibraltar Rock on your list right now and go there soon. You get a fun climb up the big rock and outrageously gorgeous views of the Wisconsin River Valley. Devil's Lake is nothing short of magical and packed with frame-worthy views. In the Glacial Plains regions near Madison, check out Lakeshore Preserve for quiet, streamside walks and panoramic views, or wander among wildflowers and wildlife at Yellowstone Lake State Park.

Quiet rest stop in the woods Denice Breaux

38 Devil's Lake State Park

Wisconsin's largest state park hosts some of the Midwest's most exquisite scenery and balcony views from high bluffs. Have it all and more on the short East Bluff Trail loop. Chase it with an optional circumnavigation of the entire lake for extra exhilarating miles.

Distance: 2.6 miles (3.1 miles if completing the spur trail to Balanced Rock)
Difficulty: Moderate
Photogenic factor: 5
Hiking time: About 2 hours
Trail surface: Hard-packed dirt and gravel path, with a short section of aged asphalt
Other trail users: None

Canine compatibility: Leashed pets allowed
Land status: State park
Fees and permits: Vehicle pass required
Maps: State park maps; USGS Baraboo
Trail contacts: Devil's Lake State Park, 55975 Park Rd., Baraboo, WI 53913; (608) 356-8301; dnr.wi.gov/topic/parks/name/devilslake

---

Finding the trailhead: From I-90/94, follow US 12 south 10 miles to exit 219 (South Boulevard). Turn left to WI 136 and head south 3 miles to the park entrance. **Trailhead GPS:** N43 42.844' / W89 72.655'

The Hike

Nearly 2 billion years in the making, the Baraboo Hills were at one time higher than the Rockies, and as is common throughout much of Wisconsin, ice played a big role in the lumpy topography we see today. The dramatic 500-foot bluffs surrounding Devil's Lake were sculpted by a monstrously thick glacier, and the lake itself formed by terminal moraines that plugged gaps in the bluffs at the north and south ends. Incredible. I'm forever fascinated by the unfathomable power of glaciers and find myself thinking about ice every time I hike in this area.

The stop-in-your-tracks beauty of this place appeals to lots of other people as well. From the start of the twentieth century, in fact, the area has attracted hordes of visitors, and today, more than 1 million visitors a year pour into the park. The good news is it's relatively easy to steer clear of the throngs via trails less traveled. Even better news is the park is also packed with around 100 bird species, nearly 900 plant species, and a star-studded cast of Wisconsin mammals, such as white-tailed deer, gray wolves, flying squirrels, red foxes, various raptors, coyotes, rabbits, and beavers.

From the trailhead, follow the wide dirt path/road southeast to the junction with the East Bluff Woods Trail. Veer left and start climbing through a wildly scenic maple-mixed hardwood forest. There's a full mile and 500 feet of elevation gain ahead of you, so just settle into a comfortable rhythm and enjoy this beautiful place.

Great views of Devil's Lake from the top of the east ridge DENICE BREAUX

After trekking across the top of the bluff, you'll reach a junction with the Balanced Rock Trail. It's only about 0.2 mile (but fairly steep) to this remarkable geologic oddity and worth the trip if you're up for it. To find the rock, turn left and start climbing. Head back down when you're done and follow the East Bluff Trail. Linger at the overlooks for outrageous views of mile-long Devil's Lake far below. *Note:* Be careful! A moment of inattention or a misstep can lead to a long fall and bad things will happen. Enjoy the views safely.

From here, the East Bluff Trail begins a long descent with a few relatively steep sections on its way to the valley floor and the junction left back to the trailhead.

Why Go?

It's Tolkien's world come to life at Parfrey's Glen, Wisconsin's first State Natural Area. Located in the southwest corner of Devil's Lake State Park, Parfrey's is a deep, ragged slash, up to 100 feet in places, in the Baraboo Hills sandstone. The glen is highlighted by striated cliff walls emblazoned with emerald-green moss dripping from consistent water seepage and cool temperatures. The favorable conditions also host northern-centric tree and plant species, including yellow birch and red elder, along with a fast-running stream and small waterfall. It is one our state's brightest gems (in the shade) and attracts hordes of visitors every year.

Beautiful hiking along the ridge DENICE BREAUX

Miles and Directions

0.0   From the trailhead, hike southeast on the dirt road.

0.1   Reach junction with the East Bluff Woods Trail, veer left.

1.4   At the junction with Balanced Rock Trail, turn left and descend to see the rock. The main route turns right, climbing for a short distance to several overlooks with life-list views of Devil's Lake and the west and south bluffs. Descend on East Bluff Trail.

2.5   Arrive at the hike's first junction with the East Bluff Woods Trail. Turn left to return to the trailhead.

2.6   Arrive back at the trailhead.

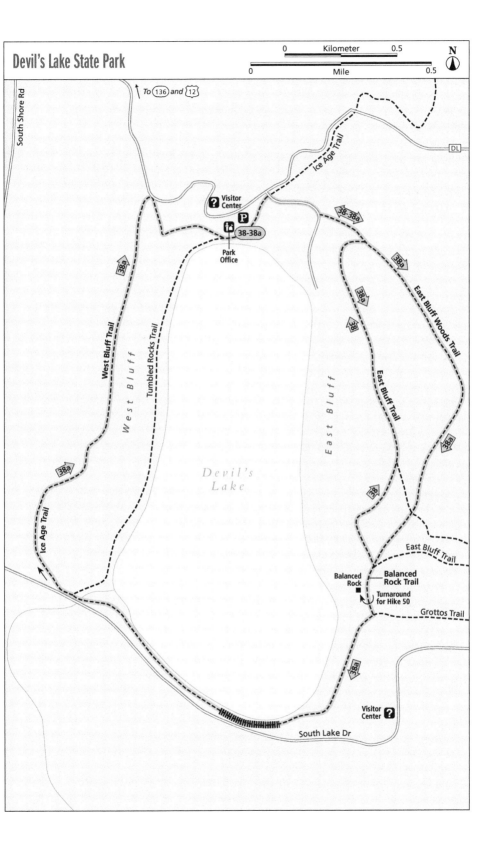

Devil's Lake State Park

0   Kilometer   0.5

0   Mile   0.5

N

To 136 and 12

South Shore Rd

Ice Age Trail

DL

Visitor Center

P

38-38a

Park Office

38-38a

38a

38a

East Bluff Woods Trail

West Bluff Trail

West Bluff

Tumbled Rocks Trail

38a

38

East Bluff Trail

East Bluff

38a

38a

Devil's Lake

Ice Age Trail

38a

38

East Bluff Trail

Balanced Rock

Balanced Rock Trail

Turnaround for Hike 50

Grottos Trail

38a

Visitor Center

South Lake Dr

38a Bonus Hike: Devil's Lake Roundabout

Distance: 5.1 miles
Difficulty: Challenging

Hiking time: About 3 hours

Finding the trailhead: Trailhead GPS: From I-90/94, follow US 12 south 10 miles to exit 219 (South Boulevard). Turn left to WI 136 and head south 3 miles to the park entrance. **Trailhead GPS:** N43 42.844' / W89 72.655'

The Hike

For the adventurous spirit, it's tough to resist making a day of it on a circumnavigation of the lake, taking in lofty views from the soaring east and west bluffs. From the same trailhead as the East Bluff hike above, follow the East Bluff Trail southbound to Balanced Rock and at the Grottos Trail junction, veer right to loop past the tangle of concession stands and lots of people at the lake's south shore.

A short section of boardwalk angles up toward the boat ramp and the junction with the Tumbled Rocks and West Bluff Trails. Follow the West Bluff Trail up a long grade to the top and plan on stopping many times to ogle outrageously beautiful views of the lake and rolling hills to the east. The trail squiggles up for a while before eventually descending to North Shore Road. A right turn here leads past the northern beach and concessions, with a final curve back north and east to the trailhead.

Miles and Directions

0.0 From the trailhead, hike southeast on the dirt road.

0.1 Reach junction with the East Bluff Woods Trail, turn right.

1.2 Reach junction with the Balanced Rock Trail, turn right and descend to see the rock.

1.6 Reach junction with the Grottos Trail, turn right and hike past the south-shore area.

3.0 Merge with the West Bluff Trail and start a long, steady climb to the top of the bluff. (This is also part of the Ice Age Trail.)

4.4 Reach junction with North Shore Road, turn right and follow the trail past the beach to the upper parking areas and the east trailhead.

5.1 Arrive back at the trailhead.

39 Natural Bridge State Park

One of America's six Natural Bridge State Parks, this one features an arch dating to 12,000 years ago, a blend of forest and prairie, and showy wildflowers.

Distance: 2.6 miles, with options for additional miles
Difficulty: Easy
Photogenic factor: 4
Hiking time: About 75 minutes
Trail surface: Hard packed dirt
Other trail users: None
Canine compatibility: Leashed pets allowed

Land status: State park
Fees and permits: Vehicle pass required
Maps: State park map; USGS Black Hawk
Trail contacts: Natural Bridge State Park, E7792 CR C, North Freedom, WI 53951; (608) 356-8301; dnr.wi.gov/topic/parks/name/naturalbridge

Finding the trailhead: From Baraboo, follow US 12 south 8 miles to CR C. Turn right and head west 10 miles to the park entrance on the right. **Trailhead GPS:** N43 20.425' / W89 55.488'

The Hike

Census records from the early 1900s show the family of German immigrants Carl and Johanna Raddatz as occupants of a farm on the land of today's Natural Bridge State Park. While that was a long time ago indeed, evidence from the land itself confirms they were not the first to settle here. Wisconsin Historical Society studies in 1957 revealed charred wood dating between 9,000 and 8,000 B.C., the oldest human occupancy in the upper Midwest. Experts believe the stone arch we see today was used periodically as a shelter or seasonal camp and later more formally inhabited. Imagine life in Wisconsin with enormous glaciers in the background!

Scoured and carved by tirelessly swirling water and wind, the sandstone arch's portal is currently an ample 25 feet high and 35 feet wide, the largest in the state. It will look decidedly different in generations to come, but for now it's our version of the legendary arch monuments in Utah and other parts west. The park includes more than 500 acres and hosts a 60-acre scientific study area among dense hardwood forest

100 YEARS OF BARSTOOLS

Leland, just one mile southwest of Natural Bridge State Park, is the classic old Wisconsin townscape of a couple of bars, a church, and a handful of houses. One of those bars is Sprecher's, with a long wooden bar soaked in a century of history. Edwin Sprecher's father bought the place in 1900 as a general store during Prohibition, eventually transforming it to a bar. They've been serving up frosty mugs ever since.

Sunlight on the arch DENICE BREAUX

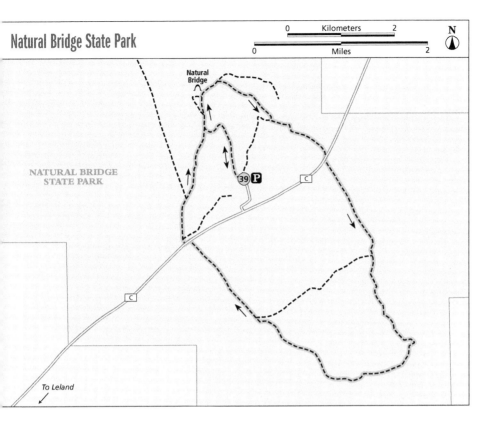

0   Kilometers   2

0   Miles   2

N

Natural
Bridge

NATURAL BRIDGE
STATE PARK

39 P

C

C

C

To Leland

littered with flora, such as the slender lip fern, walking fern, and the rare purple cliff brake. Visitors are also treated to meadows packed with wildflowers and patches of open prairie. Four miles of trails wander through the park in a lopsided loop and hikers are sure to see some of the resident critters, including deer, turkey, the usual skittering squirrels, woodpeckers, and bald eagles. An intriguing 1890 log house still stands near the highway, as well as remnants of a stone smokehouse and adjacent homesite.

Start this clockwise loop heading north, directly to the arch bridge. It's plenty impressive but sort of "hides" among the foliage in summer, like it's just part of the natural way of things. Fall is my favorite time to hike here, with golden leaves and crisp, quiet days. Just past the bridge is an optional, short side trip on the Indian Moccasin Nature Trail and a picture-worthy overlook. On the main loop, the fern-lined path maintains a southeasterly trajectory through the woods and across the highway to patches of open, flowery meadow. You'll pass a short-cut trail along the way and then make a wide curve back northwest to cross the highway again. A couple of side trails invite additional exploring, but the main loop is a straightforward, delightful hike in the Wisconsin countryside.

One ding in an otherwise enjoyable stroll is relatively poor signage. Getting lost and scavenging for food and shelter is hardly a concern, but you might find yourself backtracking now and again to reorient on the right path.

Trailside wildflowers DENICE BREAUX

Why Go?

The arch bridge itself lies within the Natural Bridge and Rockshelter State Natural Area, a place of fascinating study and exploration of times long ago. Mollusk species were discovered here as well as special interest remains of everything from passenger pigeon to bobcat and pine marten to mountain lion. Prairie remnants are small but contain Indian grass, little blue-stem, and other prairie grasses. Look to the shaded cliff areas for unusual walking fern, named for their ability to sprout new plantlets wherever arching leaves of a parent plant touch the ground.

Miles and Directions

0.0   Hike north from the trailhead, following signage to the natural bridge.

0.2   Turn right to the arch bridge.

0.3   Pass the Indian Moccasin Nature Trail, continue southeast on main trail.

1.0   Cross CR C.

1.2   Pass shortcut trail on the right.

1.9   Pass the other end of the short-cut trail.

2.1   Cross CR C again.

2.4   Turn right to return to the trailhead.

2.6   Arrive back at the trailhead.

40 Wildcat Mountain State Park

This short lollipop loop follows the gentle coulee curves and hills of one of Wisconsin's most revered river valleys. A state natural area within the park hosts 400-year-old hemlocks and the deep gorge is a fairy tale come true for canoeists.

Distance: 2.5-mile lollipop
Difficulty: Moderate
Photogenic factor: 5
Hiking time: About 75 minutes
Trail surface: Hard packed dirt
Other trail users: None
Canine compatibility: Leashed pets allowed

Land status: State park
Fees and permits: Vehicle pass required
Maps: State park map; USGS Ontario
Trail contacts: Wildcat Mountain State Park, E13660 WI 33, Ontario, WI 54651; (608) 337-4775; dnr.wi.gov/topic/parks/name/wildcat

Finding the trailhead: From Ontario, head southeast on WI 33 for 2.4 miles to the park entrance on the left. **Trailhead GPS:** N43 41.513' / W90 34.260'

The Hike

It's not *all* about milk and cheese here in Wisconsin. Did you know the Kickapoo River Valley is one of the world's largest producers of ginseng? The coulees hereabouts provide ideal growing conditions for this revered medicinal root. The valley is also a magic kingdom for hiking and other outdoor adventure pursuits, and some of the best trails to lay down boot tracks are in Wildcat Mountain State Park. This park boasts an impressive 3,500 acres and many miles of hiking trails, including the short, flat Prairie Trail; Ice Cave Trail; the Hemlock Trail, which winds through an ancient, emerald-green valley; and the Old Settler's Trail, featured here.

Entirely appropriate for a river of such squiggly inclinations, "kickapoo" in Algonquin means "that which goes here, then there." Indeed, the earliest American Indians traveling and living in this exquisite place named this "the river of canoes," a title still

HEMLOCKS AND HARDWOODS

Within Wildcat Mountain State Park is the Mount Pisgah Hemlock–Hardwoods State Natural Area, which features a reverent stand of ancient hemlock and yellow birch flanking the Kickapoo River. Stands of white oak and white pine join the display and the adjacent cliff faces are home to uncommon plant species dating to preglacial times, including the Louisiana waterthrush and Sullivan's cool-wort. Rare birds such as Kentucky and Cerulean warblers and Acadian flycatchers also live in the valley.

Trail through the tall pines DENICE BREAUX

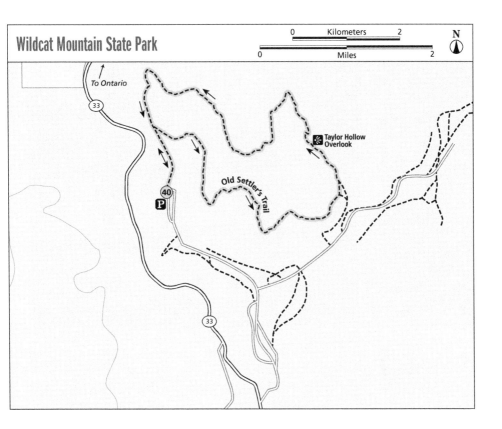

Wildcat Mountain State Park

0   Kilometers   2

0   Miles   2

N

To Ontario

33

Taylor Hollow Overlook

40

P

Old Settler's Trail

33

held high by modern-day paddlers. The Kickapoo tours 126 miles of idyllic country-side on its way to the Wisconsin River, dropping nearly 350 feet through high, striated sandstone bluffs closely resembling those of the Wisconsin Dells. This exceedingly beautiful environment, especially near and on Mount Pisgah, hosts vibrant stands of enormous hemlock and pine, spared from the logging era's scourge and subsequent overgrazing of various livestock. Some of these giants are 400 years old, with 6-foot diameter trunks supporting 200 feet of majestic life. Virgin timber like this is a rarity these days and inspired a designation of the Mount Pisgah Hemlock–Hardwoods State Natural Area within the state park.

The humid environment of the river gorge sprouts tapestries of mosses and ferns, and dozens of bird species live here or migrate through, including tundra swans, great blue herons, bald eagles, red-tailed hawks, and sandpipers. You'll have a chance to see those critters and more along the Old Settler's Trail.

Start the hike near the park office, where you'll encounter an initial descent as you travel past the upper picnic area to the start of the loop proper. Follow the trail to the right as it passes through pine stands planted by Ontario students. The trailside amphitheater offers an otherworldly view of the valley and Ontario in far distance. The trail winds through dense hardwood forest for the most part, with sections of wooden log stairs on steeper climbs.

Taylor Hollow Overlook DENICE BREAUX

About halfway through the loop is the Taylor Hollow Overlook, which unfortunately doesn't look over much in summer months due to a green shroud of foliage. From here, the path drops into the verdant valley, crosses a stream, and lopes in and around a pair of coulees back to the stem of the loop and the return to the trailhead.

Why Go?

The Kickapoo River and smaller feeder tributaries are defined in places by significant beaver activity. A keystone species in these parts, beavers naturally boost ecosystem biodiversity by creating ponds and wetlands, increasing riparian habitats and inspiring colonization of aquatic plants. Diversity of bird, mammal, fish, and insect life is also augmented. Trumpeter swans, for example, use beaver lodges as nesting sites, and those same lodges provide homes for cavity-nesting wood ducks, mergansers, and owls.

Miles and Directions

0.0 Hike north from the trailhead on the stem of the loop.

0.2 Turn right to start the loop.

1.0 Pass the amphitheater.

1.3 Arrive at Taylor Hollow Overlook, then descend into the valley and to a stream crossing.

2.3 Reach junction with the stem trail of the loop. Continue straight ahead.

2.5 Arrive back at the trailhead.

41 Castle Mound Nature Trail

On this exhilarating hike you will find glacial-scoured Central Plain lowlands to the right, unglaciated coulee country to the left, and a direct path through a state natural area jam-packed with ancient geological highlights—all in less than 3 miles.

Distance: 2.2 miles, with two short spur trails to overlooks
Difficulty: Moderate with steeper grades to overlooks
Photogenic factor: 5
Hiking time: 60–75 minutes
Trail surface: Hard-packed dirt and grass
Other trail users: None
Canine compatibility: Pets not allowed

Land status: State forest
Fees and permits: Vehicle pass required
Maps: State forest map; USGS Black River Falls
Trail contacts: Black River State Forest, W10325 Highway 12, Black River Falls, WI 54615; (715) 284-4103; dnr.wi.gov/topic/StateForests/blackriver

Finding the trailhead: From Black River Falls, follow US 12 southeast to Castle Mound Campground and the trailhead. **Trailhead GPS:** N44 17.041' / W90 49.455'

The Hike

It's not every day you can hike to the top of a monadnock. In the vicinity of present-day Black River Falls and a busy interstate, there once was a great big mountain. The eternal artistry of wind, rain, and ice chipped away at the mountain and Castle Mound is the nearly completed sculpture; an isolated, weathering ridge called a monadnock. This one is about 400 million years old. Come back in another 100 million years or so and the ridge will look quite different or be gone altogether. Today, however, Castle Mound is one of Wisconsin's most prized features, especially spectacular with its craggy rock formations hidden among a forest of oak, pine, maple, aspen, and birch. An interesting "ecological dividing line" separates a dry pine forest on the southwest flanks of the mound and cool, wet environs on the northeast face.

Rising nearly 200 feet above the ground below, Castle Mound's central backbone is made of exposed and shaded cliffs, and huge boulders are scattered all over the place. The trail passes near, around, or over many of them, making for a lively hike. Look to the forest floor to see the likes of large-leaved aster, partridge berry, and wintergreen. Overhead are melodies and brief appearances of red-breasted nuthatches, scarlet tanagers, solitary vireos, warblers, and lots more. Up high on the summit, expect to see the silent flight of eagles, hawks, buzzards, and other raptors.

Right from the beginning, this hike has an ethereal, Middle Earth vibe. In many places the trail is colored orange with a thick layer of pine needles and the path sneaks around huge, angular boulders for most of the way. Indeed, a hobbit would feel right

Wisconsin Stonehenge DENICE BREAUX

at home, especially with nearby hideaways such as Giant's Castle and Goat's Cave. One of my favorite attractions on this trail is the huge ramp-shaped rock with a sheer face that looks as if it was cut with some kind of primordial saw. The face is covered base to peak in soft moss, with a crewcut of baby ferns on top. Another fascinating sight is a raggedy rock, the size of a Volkswagen Beetle, pockmarked with holes. Right in the middle of this rock a spindly pine tree merrily grows, its splayed roots clinging to the rock like that alien creepy from *The Thing* movie.

Farther up the trail are collections of rock towers, some of them 30 feet high with wall-straight cuts. Others look like piles of really overcooked pancakes topped with dollops of petrified whipped cream. Sentinel red pines stand in formation around these rock mini-castles, and ferns and moss grow everywhere. It's a wonderfully fantastical place and every time I come here is like the first time. The top of the mound, of course, is the main attraction for most hikers, and for good reason. A cool steel ladder leads up the final steep slope of a boulder conglomeration and the ensuing views are among the best in the state. A few tall pines flank a mural-worthy scene of tree-covered plains stretching miles to the northeastern horizon. Off to the west is the lumpy topography of the Western Coulee Region. It is mesmerizing to say the least, and in the fall looks like one big static, smoldering bed of embers.

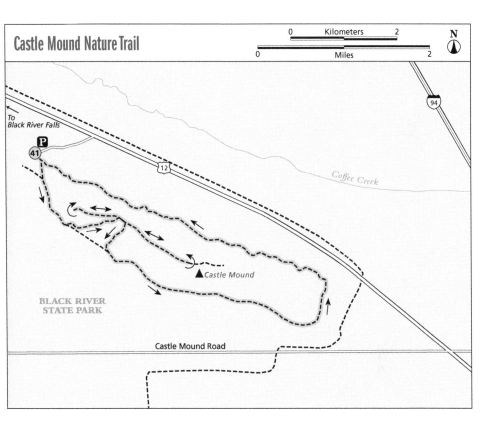

Kilometers 0 — 2

Miles 0 — 2

N

To Black River Falls

94

Coffee Creek

▲ Castle Mound

BLACK RIVER STATE PARK

Castle Mound Road

From the trailhead, take the Nature Center Trail's right fork and start a steady climb to a junction with a spur trail heading left to an overlook. Backtrack to the main trail and the climb through the woods to the ladder leading to the observation deck. After ogling the views, retreat to the junction below and turn left to complete the loop. The trail essentially follows the base of the mound around its bulbous southeastern nose to a long, straighter homestretch to the trailhead.

This is a great destination hike or perfect road trip rest stop. Access is easy, and once on the trail all you have to do is ignore the drone of traffic from I-94 and Highway 12 and imagine this place a few hundred million years ago.

Why Go?

Black River State Forest sprawls over nearly 70,000 acres and includes 12 miles of the Black River. What we see today was significantly inspired by Ice Age glaciation. The protruding rock formations of Upper Cambrian sandstone are remnants of giant mountains that eroded to ridges and buttes and knolls. Timber wolves roam the forest, wandering through rare flora such as beak grass and sand violet. The Dike 17 Wildlife Area includes a 1,300-acre waterfowl protection space composed of flowages and open landscape.

Heading up trail Denice Breaux

Miles and Directions

0.0 From the trailhead, follow the Nature Center Trail's right fork.

0.3 Turn left for a short side trip to an overlook, then retrace your tracks to the main trail and head uphill, encountering a ladder on the way, to the summit and observation deck.

0.7 Arrive at the mound summit.

0.8 Turn left to complete the loop.

2.2 Arrive back at the trailhead.

42 Wildcat Mound–Smrekar Trails

Follow boulevard-like trails on undulating terrain through quintessential Wisconsin forest dedicated solely to silent sports. Top it off with outrageous views of tidy green valleys for a perfect boots-on-the-ground getaway.

Distance: 4 miles, with options for additional miles
Difficulty: Moderate, but expect consistent ups and downs
Photogenic factor: 4
Hiking time: 90 minutes
Trail surface: Wide, grassy trail with sections of packed dirt
Other trail users: None

Canine compatibility: Leashed pets allowed
Land status: State forest
Fees and permits: None
Maps: State forest map; USGS Black River Falls
Trail contacts: Black River State Forest, W10325 Highway 12, Black River Falls, WI 54615; (715) 284-4103; dnr.wi.gov/topic/StateForests/blackriver

Finding the trailhead: From I-94 at the Millston exit, follow CR O 0.3 mile to North Settlement Road and turn left. Go 3.2 miles to Shale Road and turn left again. The trailhead is roughly 1.5 miles on the left. **Trailhead GPS:** N44 15.013' / W90 35.514'

The Hike

Given its proximity to Wisconsin's busiest interstate, you'd expect hiking trails in Black River State Forest to be crawling with people. One step into these woods and you'll be pleasantly surprised: It is anything but crowded. In fact, the only company you are likely to have will be wild critters. If you are feeling off the grid, bring your gear for some backcountry camping.

This loop traipses along 4 miles of rolling terrain on wide trails cut and maintained for cross-country skiing. (Remember that when winter comes back around. This place is sublime for skinny skis.) The trails are almost always impeccably groomed in summer, but like every other woodsy locale in this part of the country, beware of ticks and mosquitoes. They will clamp to your skin and tell all their friends to join the party. Be prepared with long pants and sleeves or, at the very least, copious applications of bug repellent.

But don't let annoying little insects spoil your day. Head through the gate at the parking area and follow a forest road north to the start of the loop. Signage at intersections is excellent, so there's no need to fear getting lost. Veer right and follow barely there elevation changes through a showy stretch of forest, with oaks competing with pines trying to outdo aspens. It's a relaxing section of the loop on the way to its top end and approximate halfway point. The path does a hairpin turn into a former oak savannah, opening to show its best look, and entices adventurous, off-trail exploring.

Rolling through the forest DENICE BREAUX

Linger-worthy views DENICE BREAUX

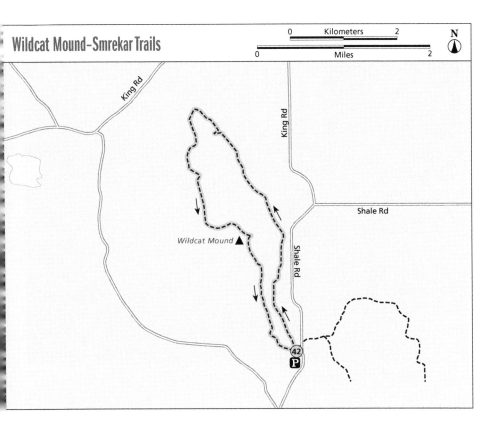

0   Kilometers   2

0   Miles   2

N

King Rd

King Rd

Shale Rd

Wildcat Mound ▲

Shale Rd

42

P

From here, plan on a steady uphill grind to the top of Wildcat Mound, where a short single-track spur trail awaits to escort you through a stand of noble oaks to an overlook of faraway views of the surrounding bucolic countryside. Secluded, quiet Wisconsin—doesn't get much better.

From the top of the mound, cruise along a ridgeline over a succession of fun rollers heading southbound. Not far from the end of the hike, you'll pass the ski shortcut trail and climb to another great lookout point with a bench conveniently staged for another rest break. It's a downhill coast from the overlook back to the trailhead. Feeling like more miles? Simply walk across the road for another 2-mile loop.

Why Go?

Wisconsin and Minnesota have made incredibly beneficial strides in the reestablishment and restoration of timber wolves to their rightful place. In fact, the Wildcat Mound area of Black River State Forest hosted the state's southernmost pack of breeding wolves as recently as the early 1990s. The Wildcat Mound group are known today as the pioneers of wolf reintroduction in Wisconsin, and a prospering elk herd has also settled into these hills and dales. Be on the lookout for a life-list glimpse of these elegant creatures.

Trailside furniture DENICE BREAUX

Miles and Directions

0.0 From the trailhead, hike north, generally paralleling Shale Road.

1.6 Reach the hairpin turn into the oak savannah.

2.6 Arrive at the top of Wildcat Mound. Follow the spur trail to the overlook.

3.3 Reach the final overlook point.

4.0 Arrive back at the trailhead.

43 Lakeshore Nature Preserve-UW Madison

Muir and Leopold were here. Put your boots on the same ground as these seminal environmentalists with a relaxing hike on Lake Mendota's postcard peninsula.

Distance: 2 miles for Picnic Point (add 0.7 mile to Frautschi Point)
Difficulty: Easy to moderate
Photogenic factor: 5
Hiking time: 1+ hour
Trail surface: Hard-packed dirt path and some paved
Other trail users: Runners

Canine compatibility: Leashed pets allowed
Land status: University of Wisconsin
Fees and permits: None
Maps: Preserve maps; USGS Madison West
Trail contacts: Lakeshore Nature Preserve, 30 N. Mills St., Madison, WI 53715; (608) 265-9275; lakeshorepreserve.wisc.edu

Finding the trailhead: From the north end of Camp Randall Stadium on the UW campus, follow University Avenue westbound 0.6 mile to Walnut Street. Turn right and follow Walnut north 0.5 mile to its junction with Willow Drive. Continue north to University Bay Drive. Turn right and head north 0.25 mile to the preserve entrance and trailhead. **Trailhead GPS:** N43 08.427' / W89 42.868'

The Hike

Maybe it's just me, but there's something special about walking the same ground as John Muir and Aldo Leopold. Both legendary environmental thinkers studied at the University of Wisconsin (UW), and their influence is alive in these woods.

Lakeshore Preserve covers 300 acres and includes more than 4 miles of splendidly scenic Lake Mendota shoreline, protecting a piece of UW-Madison's irreplaceable natural treasures. Picnic Point, the highlight of this particular hike, is a peninsula poking out nearly a full mile into Lake Mendota and arguably the most popular outdoor destination for students and Madison residents as a whole.

Today's visitors, of course, are far from the first to appreciate the area. Evidence of ancient peoples from 12,000 years ago has been found on the point, and the early nineteenth century saw several farmsteads sprout among the woods and open fields.

From the trailhead near University Bay Marsh, hike northeast through a short, narrow sliver of open area and then into a forest of mixed hardwoods that includes maple, red oak, elm, and basswood. Along the southern edge of Picnic Point, pass a couple of fire rings (favorite locales for evening social hours) and eventually reach the tip of the point. Breathtaking 180-degree views of Lake Mendota, UW's main campus, and the state capitol complex unfold from here. Loop left around the point and head back along its northern edge past Picnic Point Marsh to a junction on its

Idyllic hiking in the preserve DENICE BREAUX

western end. If you've had enough at this point, turn left (west) here and head back to the trailhead for a 2-mile hike.

For a longer (and additional 0.7 mile) loop to Frautschi Point, continue northwest along the shore, enjoying intermittent views of the lake through the dense woods. With the exception of a few gradual elevation changes, this stretch is fairly level and easygoing. You'll pass through Caretaker's Woods, an 8-acre patch of forest immediately east of Biocore Prairie. This land was once part of the sprawling estate of Edward Young, and his caretaker lived in a little house at the edge of the property, hence the name. The caretaker kept busy pruning the orchard, clearing snow, and keeping an eye on sneaky university students. The home's aged foundations are still visible today. Notice that some of the big oaks have wide-reaching branches. This is evidence that in their younger years they grew in a more open environment, which indeed this area was before the forest proper took over. Don't miss the opportunity to stroll to the top of the hill for beauteous views of Lake Mendota.

Once you're ready, follow the path northwest through Second Point Woods and on to Frautschi Point, the large nose of land poking out in the lake. The generous gift of this parcel to the university in the late 1980s linked the university's portion of the shoreline and made the creation of the Lakeshore Nature Preserve possible.

Lakeshore Nature Preserve—UW Madison

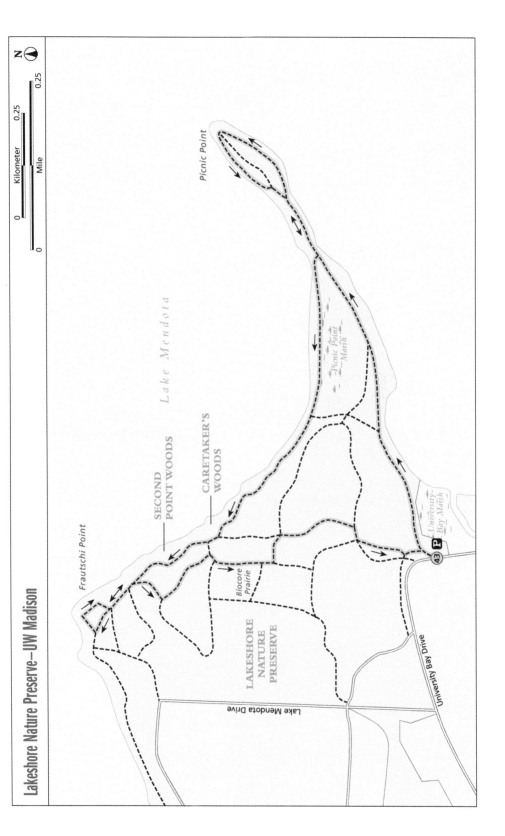

Family hiking in a shaded forest DENICE BREAUX

Enjoy the point for a while and then squiggle down the path through the east side of the prairie to return to the trailhead.

Why Go?

Natural resources and related studies are a big deal at the University of Wisconsin–Madison. Students and faculty have closely studied and monitored flora and fauna of Lakeshore Preserve for more than a century. In fact, the ecosystem comprising University Bay is arguably the most researched in the country. Seminal restoration projects nurtured the plant communities we see today, including restoring the Muir Woods ground story and transforming reclaimed cornfield into marshland. The tradition continues with a combined student-researcher effort to reestablish an old field to native prairie.

Miles and Directions

0.0   From the trailhead, hike northeast along the point.

0.6   Reach a split in the trail, turn right to make a counterclockwise loop around the skinny point.

Relaxing up close with Lake Mendota DENICE BREAUX

1.0 Veer right at this junction.

1.6 Reach the junction for Picnic Point Marsh; turn left for the shorter loop back to the trailhead. (See directions below for the longer option).

2.0 Arrive back at the trailhead.

Longer Frautschi Point Loop Option (directions from mile 1.6 above)

1.6 For the longer option, turn right at the junction with the Picnic Point Marsh trail, and follow it along the lakeshore.

1.8 Turn right here on the short horseshoe trail at the tip of the point and right again on the other side.

1.9 Turn left here and right at the next fork just ahead.

2.0 Left turn at this junction and right at the next.

2.1 Turn right.

2.3 Turn right (south), passing all side trails to 2.5 miles.

2.5 Turn right.

2.6 Turn right back to the trailhead.

2.7 Arrive back at the trailhead.

44 University of Wisconsin Arboretum

This is a 1,200-acre sanctuary with decades of conservation efforts and inspiration from none other than Aldo Leopold. It's all here at the University of Wisconsin's Arboretum, tailor made for wandering, connecting, and simply being.

Distance: 1.8 miles, with options for additional miles
Difficulty: Easy
Photogenic factor: 4+
Hiking time: About 1 hour
Trail surface: Packed dirt and grass
Other trail users: None
Canine compatibility: Pets not allowed

Land status: University of Wisconsin
Fees and permits: None
Maps: UW Arboretum maps; USGS Madison West
Trail contacts: UW Arboretum, 1207 Seminole Hwy., Madison, WI 53711; (608) 263-7888; arboretum.wisc.edu

Finding the trailhead: From I-90, follow US 12 for 7 miles to South Park Street and curve south just over 0.5 mile to Haywood Drive. Turn right and go 3 blocks to North Wingra Drive and head straight across to Arboretum Drive. Follow the road 1.8 miles to the parking area on the right. **Trailhead GPS:** N43 04.557' / W89 42.763'

The Hike

What began as an effort to preserve open space and provide a quiet place to escape the city eventually inspired the entirely new idea of ecological restoration, driven in large part by the commitment of Aldo Leopold. One of the most influential figures in environmental ethics and the wilderness conservation movement, Leopold's ideals are alive on the pages of *A Sand County Almanac*, widely regarded as the most important book on the environment ever published. He was also a founding member of the Wilderness Society, a professor of game management at UW, and a proponent of a vibrant arboretum with a focus on reestablishing original Wisconsin landscapes such as oak savannas and tallgrass prairies.

To that end, for 6 years beginning in 1935, crews from the Civilian Conservation Corps (CCC) worked tirelessly to begin restoring the area's natural ecosystems, and the Arb today includes more than 1,200 acres in Madison, as well as out-of-state locations, all working to preserve land and restore ecological communities. With such esteemed lineage and decades of successful environmental efforts, it's hard not to be filled with pride and gratitude walking these trails.

From the Wingra Springs parking area, follow the path north past ancient effigy mounds. Follow the path north and west as it leads to the N5 trail marker for a great, up-close view of Big Spring and its perpetual flow into the lake. Hike east from here to K4, turn right (south) through splendiferous Wingra Woods. The trail reaches the

Trail running at the Arb DENICE BREAUX

road crossing and then gently curves to G5 and a left turn into the enchanting Lost City Forest. The trail wanders through here to L4 and a right turn bends around to L3. Go right again, pass F2, and hike along Juniper Knoll (don't miss a quick side trip on the short path to Teal Pond on the right) to F6. From here the trail heads due north between Gallistel Woods and the visitor center garden areas. At G7, take the short spur trail left and cross the road back to the trailhead.

I have a hunch you'd like to see more of this wonderful place, and you're in luck because the Arb has 15 more miles of trails to explore. No trip here is complete without touring the visitor center or tagging along on a guided tour of the gardens.

THE GARDENS

The UW Arboretum delights the senses with three outrageously beautiful and ecologically diverse garden areas, including an inspiring example of a wildly successful native plant community restoration. Highlighting the field is the 35-acre Longenecker Horticultural Garden, internationally known for its 2,500 different plant species and North America's largest display of lilacs. The Viburnum Garden hosts 3 acres and nearly 100 species of its namesake plant and 110 of arborvitae. The Wisconsin Native Plant Garden includes fifteen separate gardens with hundreds of native plant species and fascinating displays of ecological restoration.

Fall color hiking DENICE BREAUX

Why Go?

It's no secret that insect pollinators are vital to natural ecosystems and agricultural processes, and yet application of pesticides and destruction of pollinator habitat continues unabated. Native, wild bees are highly diverse in a variety of habitats and provide critical (and free) pollination services. The UW Arboretum is one of the endangered rusty patched bumble bees' few remaining habitats. This unique position inspired researchers to leverage the Arb's outdoor "lab" to study targeted photography in identifying pollinators and assist land managers in tracking the range and habitat use of these irreplaceable species.

Miles and Directions

0.0 From the trailhead, hike north in and around the effigy mounds and then follow the path northwest to trail marker N5 for a look at Big Spring. Continue the route east from here.

0.3 At the junction with trail marker K4, turn right (south) to pass through Wingra Woods.

0.6 Reach a road crossing at Arboretum Drive.

0.7 At the junction with trail marker G5, turn left to drop down through Lost City Forest.

1.1 At the junction with marker L4, turn right again on L3, then follow F2 (along Juniper Knoll and past Teal Pond), F3, F4,, and F6.

1.5 At the junction with marker F7, turn right and skirt the arboretum's visitor center gardens on your left, passing through Gallistel Woods.

1.7 At the junction with marker G7, turn left to cross the road and reach the trailhead.

1.8 Arrive back at the trailhead.

University of Wisconsin Arboretum

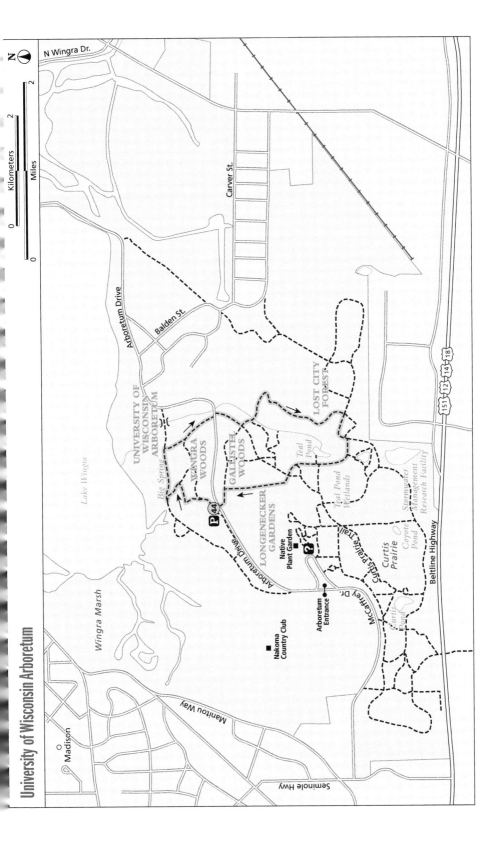

45 New Glarus Woods State Park

A rolling, woodsy bonanza accessible via two Wisconsin state trails for bike-hike outings. The village of New Glarus, America's Little Switzerland, is loaded with Swiss-inspired architecture and events.

Distance: 1.3 miles, with options for additional miles
Difficulty: Easy to moderate
Photogenic factor: 4
Hiking time: 30–40 minutes
Trail surface: Hard-packed dirt
Other trail users: None
Canine compatibility: Leashed pets allowed

Land status: State park
Fees and permits: Vehicle pass required
Maps: State park maps; USGS New Glarus
Trail contacts: New Glarus Woods State Park, W5446 Highway NN, New Glarus, WI 53574; (608) 527-2335; https://dnr.wisconsin.gov/topic/parks/ngwoods

Finding the trailhead: From New Glarus, follow WI 69 for 2 miles south to Highway NN and turn right. The park entrance is 150 yards on the right. Follow the road to the group campsite area and trailhead. **Trailhead GPS:** N42 47.134' / W89 37.465'

The Hike

This southern Wisconsin park was established in 1934, after intensive earthen sculpting by mile-thick glaciers 10,000 years earlier. Rolling hills vibrant with meadow grasses and fertile soil were created, while forests grew in hillier land. New Glarus was established in the transition area between the two.

Paleo-Indians, ancestors of early aboriginal tribes, were the first to colonize Wisconsin, hunting musk oxen, elk, bison, and other large animals in the shadow of retreating ice sheets. Among the dozens of later American Indian tribes settling in the state, several regularly used ridgetop trails for their high vantage points. One such trail ran through the middle of today's New Glarus Woods, steadily widening as European settlers plied the route with ox carts and other trade supplies. The "path" became known as the Old Lead Road, one of the original corridors between Lake Michigan and the Mississippi River. The Old Lead Road is present-day Highway NN.

When Swiss immigrants first settled here, New Glarus Woods sprawled over thousands of acres, akin to Germany's Black Forest. How did these intrepid souls wind up in Wisconsin? In 1845, two "scouts" sent from the village of Glarus, Switzerland, found this part of the state reminiscent of their home and purchased land to establish a new village in America. Later that year, the first group of settlers, 108 in all, rolled in on wagons to start a brand-new life.

They brought culture, diet, lifestyle, and grand architecture with flower-filled balconies and murals painted on town walls. This rich history shaped New Glarus's

Quiet and secluded is the order of the day

Two-tone oak leaves

earliest years and continues today, especially in rousing gatherings like the Wilhelm Tell Festival and, of course, Oktoberfest. Early settlers were hard workers as well, some of whom headed up the hill south of town to cut trees in the area of today's state park. Much of the lumber became ingredients for barrels destined to haul cheese (what else?) by rail to faraway regions of the country. Modern-day hikers can see elder trees, 250 years old and climbing, on steeper hills that were spared the ax.

Start this hike on one of those hills, adjacent to the group camp sites, descending gently to the unsigned Havenridge Nature Trail in a shallow valley on the eastern border of an old farmstead. The path is wide and expertly maintained, making for a pleasant walk in the woods. The park is especially resplendent in fall, with trees and understory foliage dressed in reds and yellow-orange.

OKTOBERFEST

In addition to fascinating destinations like the Swiss Historical Village and Swiss Center of North America, New Glarus is home to a wildly popular salute to its home country. Oktober-fest is a three-day extravaganza of all things Switzerland, with rousing music, delectable eats, wagon rides, all manner of family and kids activities, and, of course, plenty of delicious beer. Put this one on your bucket list.

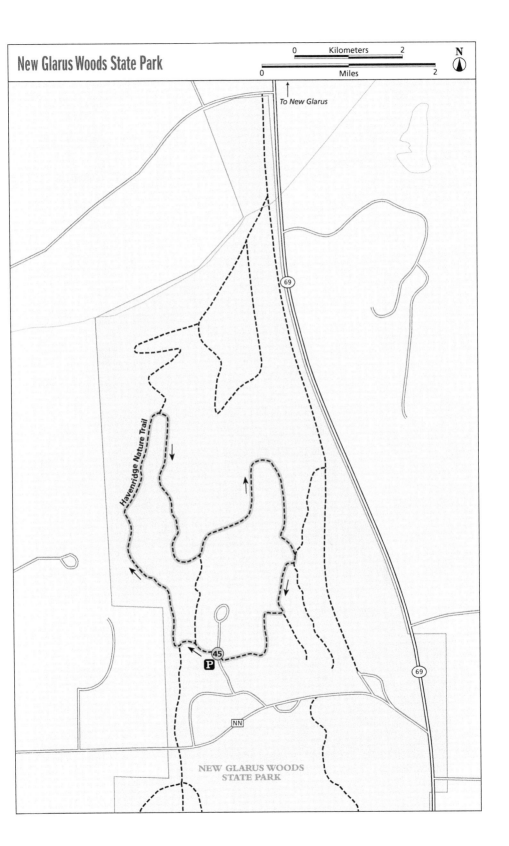

New Glarus Woods State Park

0   Kilometers   2
0   Miles   2

N

To New Glarus

69

Havenridge Nature Trail

45

P

69

NN

NEW GLARUS WOODS
STATE PARK

Fall colors on the trail

Follow the first section of trail along barely-there undulations to a buttonhook turn at the top of the loop and then southbound to another curve north. Be on the lookout for ubiquitous songbirds, white-tailed deer, grouse, and other resident critters. Most of all, the forest is a very quiet place, a homegrown elixir for all that ails ya. Sit on a log for a touch of spiritual reflection or hike all day on the extended loops north and south of the campground. Both directions lead to areas of remnant prairie and are excellent destinations to see pheasant, butterflies, dozens of bird species, and colorful wildflowers. The southern prairie offers a wildlife observation blind to get you even closer to the action.

When the trail heads southeast within earshot of Highway 69, and adjacent to the paved bike path, veer right on the Basswood Nature Trail and Chattermark Trail, gradually dropping into a tidy clearing with a rustic amphitheater that hosts various interpretive programs and related group presentations. From here it's a short climb back to the trailhead. And don't miss the park's connector path into town (hike it or bike), where delectable grub and refreshments await at a Swiss-inspired orbit of restaurants and pubs. If you're of a biking mind, the Sugar River State Trail is right here, offering a 24-mile tour of idyllic Wisconsin countryside. I've you're really ambitious, connect to the Badger State Trail near Madison and cruise 40 miles south to the state line.

This hike scores big bonus points because the north end of the park is right across the road from New Glarus Brewing Company, one of Wisconsin's pride-and-joy craft breweries. Don't miss it for a post-hike tour and suds.

Why Go?

To date, nearly 100 acres of native prairie have been restored and more than 10,000 trees planted, complementing the 250-year-old patriarchs in the park. In fact, New Glarus is known as Tree City, USA, by the National Arbor Day Foundation, thanks to continued tree-planting efforts by area residents and the commitment to the community's beloved forests. The village's annual Arbor Day Tree Planting brings the town together and to date, nearly 700 new trees have taken root in parks and open spaces.

Miles and Directions

0.0 Hike down the hill to the Havenridge Nature Trail (unsigned) and head north.

0.4 At a rest stop bench, pass the junction with the prairie trail and loop back south (right), then north (left) again 0.2 mile later.

1.0 Pass junction with a connector trail to the bike path, turn right (south) on the B trail (Basswood Nature Trail).

1.1 Turn right on the C trail (Chattermark), passing the amphitheater on the left at the bottom of the hill.

1.3 Arrive back at the trailhead.

46 Blue Mound State Park

This wildlife-packed park boasts 100-foot cliffs, a bison herd grazing on tallgrass prairie, easy access to the Military Ridge State Trail, and miles of family-friendly hiking trails.

Distance: 1.6 miles, with options for additional miles
Difficulty: Easy to moderate
Photogenic factor: 4
Hiking time: 40–50 minutes
Trail surface: Hard-packed dirt
Other trail users: None
Canine compatibility: Leashed pets allowed

Land status: State park
Fees and permits: Vehicle pass required
Maps: State park maps; USGS Blue Mounds
Trail contacts: Blue Mound State Park, 4350 Mounds Park Rd., Blue Mounds, WI 53517; (608) 437-5711; dnr.wisconsin.gov/topic/parks/bluemound

Finding the trailhead: From Mount Horeb, follow Main Street southeast to CR ID. Continue west on CR ID for 5 miles to Mounds Road. Turn right and head north 0.8 mile to the park entrance. Park near the Flint Rock Nature Trail to start the hike. **Trailhead GPS:** N43 01.433' / W89 51.081'

The Hike

Did you know that Wisconsin was once home to vast mountain ranges akin to the Alps? Granite bedrock foundations are all that remains after millions of years of erosion by ancient inland oceans and unfathomable power of the glaciers scraping across the land. This slow-motion construction/destruction cycle sliced off much of Wisconsin's iron-tough Niagara dolomite, except in places like Blue Mound State Park, where the burly rock held strong over eons, creating the mound we see today, known as a monadnock.

Blue Mound is southern Wisconsin's highest point, at 1,719 feet. It's a great place for a park, and this one boasts more than 1,100 acres with stunning views and fascinating geology. It is also where Dane County's first European settler built a small cabin (the area's first structure) and established roots of a new generation. For a while, early settlers shared this area with large and vibrant animal populations, including bobcats, timber wolves, black bears, lynx, cougars, bison, and lots more. As human numbers inexorably increased, those regal species gradually vanished, and the largest of today's resident animals are white-tailed deer, accompanied by turkey, weasels, skunks, squirrels, red and gray foxes, bats, woodchucks, raccoons, and an occasional badger.

The air above is lively with active and plentiful bird species, the most dramatic being the pileated woodpecker with its funky spiked hairdo and loud wucka-wucka-wucka call. In contrast, the wood thrush sings a much mellower, relaxing tune, while fast-twitch songbirds such as chickadees, nuthatches, ovenbirds, and finches chatter

A showy autumn forest

Lofty views from the top of the mound

the day away. In warmer months, look skyward for red-tailed hawks, bald eagles, and turkey vultures. All told, the park is the permanent or migratory home to more than 150 bird species. Don't miss their appearance in great numbers during spring and fall migrations.

Start this hike between the park's two 40-foot observation towers and be sure to make the climb to the top for otherworldly views of the Wisconsin countryside. Adjacent to the west tower, head into the woods on the Flint Rock Nature Trail, veering right at the intersection with the campground spur trail, descending steadily on hard-packed tread decorated with rocks of various shapes and sizes. The surrounding forest is absolutely stunning in any season, especially so in autumn when it feels like you're walking through clouds of floating embers.

Near the bottom of the hill the trail passes a big, misshapen boulder pitted with holes and lined with fossil patterns from a long, long time ago. From here, follow the trail along a flatter stretch and then a series of gentle undulations on the mound's northern flank. In spring and summer, this is where you'll find sizable fern species and flowering plants abundant in our state's northern pine forests, such as starflower

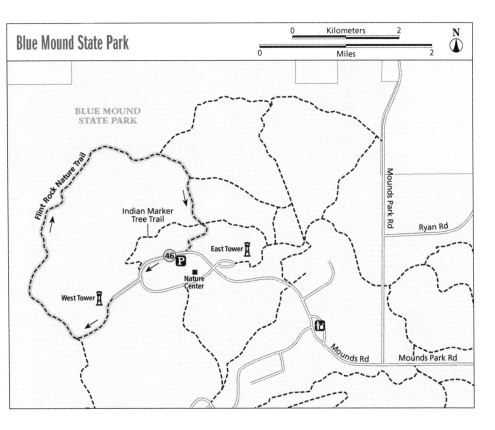

BLUE MOUND
STATE PARK

Flint Rock Nature Trail

Indian Marker
Tree Trail

East Tower

46 P

West Tower

Nature
Center

Mounds Park Rd

Ryan Rd

Mounds Rd

Mounds Park Rd

0   Kilometers   2

0   Miles   2

N

and blueberry, a hiker favorite for on-the-go snacks. The mound's east side is loaded with showy plants as well, watch for trillium, spring beauty, fawn lily, and yellow lady's slipper. Out on surrounding prairies, hikers are treated to waves of big bluestem and Indian grass, sunflowers, asters, compass plant, coneflowers, and many more.

The homestretch of the Flint Rock Nature Trail follows a moderate grade past the junction with the Indian Marker Tree Trail to a few final switchbacks back to the trailhead. Exhilarated from the hike's woodsy terrain, take a moment to consider this place in winter. If you enjoy snowshoeing or cross-country skiing, Blue Mound is a veritable playground when the ground is covered in white. Groomed trails and a warming shelter make this a go-to favorite in winter. And don't miss the nearby Military Ridge State Trail in warmer months, a popular rail-trail linking Dodgeville and Madison.

Why Go?

August 4, 1939, was a big day on the Brigham Farm. The Brigham family had farmed the land for well over a century, transforming part of it into a limestone quarry in 1903. Three decades and change later, a contractor secured by Dane County's highway department set blasting powder cartridges that subsequently shredded 5,000 tons

Radiant red maple at trailside

The fossil rock

of rock, exposing an enormous cave. A few workers accompanied Charles Brigham Jr. into the maw and discovered narrow passageways, caverns, and all manner of mysterious underground rock formations. The cave soon became a tourist attraction and Cave of the Mounds was designated a National Natural Landmark in 1988. The site continues conservation efforts today and communication of America's heritage.

Miles and Directions

0.0 Start the hike between the park's east and west observation towers, hiking into the woods on the Flint Rock Nature Trail.

0.4 Veer right at the junction with the campground spur trail. Pass the fossil boulder near the bottom of the hill.

1.5 Pass the intersection with Indian Marker Tree Trail.

1.6 Arrive back at the trailhead.

47 Yellowstone Lake State Park

Start lakeside and climb easy with the company of old-growth burr oak to stellar valley views from the ridgetop on this scenic trail in the heart of the park.

Distance: 2.4 miles, with options for additional miles
Difficulty: Moderate
Photogenic factor: 4+
Hiking time: 1 hour
Trail surface: Hard-packed dirt and grass
Other trail users: None
Canine compatibility: Leashed pets allowed

Land status: State park
Fees and permits: Vehicle pass required
Maps: State park maps; USGS Yellowstone Lake
Trail contacts: Yellowstone Lake State Park, 8495 N Lake Rd., Blanchardville, WI 53516; (608) 523-4427; dnr.wisconsin.gov/topic/parks/yellowstone

Finding the trailhead: From Mineral Point, follow WI 23 south 7.3 miles to CR G and turn left. Follow CR G east 4.7 miles to CR F and turn left. Follow CR F/D 1.7 miles and go north on F 2.1 miles to North Lake Road. Turn right; the park entrance station is 0.6 mile on the right. Start the hike at the third parking area on the left. **Trailhead GPS:** N42 46.018' / W89 58.073'

The Hike

In contrast to much of the American West, we have few manufactured reservoirs in Wisconsin. Yellowstone Lake is an exception, created between 1947 and 1954 with a dike and dam on a tributary of the Pecatonica River. State-sponsored programs helped landowners learn conservation methods to mitigate soil loss into the lake, and fish biologists conducted extensive studies on fish populations and habitat. The dam's gates were closed in June 1954, forming a new 2.5-mile-long lake. At 455 acres, the lake today is alive with bass, walleye, northern pike, panfish, muskie, bluegill, perch, and others. The western shore is a designated waterfowl refuge, a favorite migration stop for wood ducks, mallards, and geese. It is also home to resident sandhill cranes and great blue herons.

Yellowstone Lake is the summer home to more than 4,000 little brown bats that roost in thirty-one bat houses throughout the park. A dedicated local volunteer maintains the houses and the bats' voracious appetites keeps the park's mosquito population in check, a big attraction for human visitors. Other winged park residents or migratory visitors include nearly 200 bird species, including melodious songbirds, double-crested cormorant, and loon, as well as osprey, hawks, and bald eagles on the lake.

The 1,000-acre park boasts nine picnic areas, well over a hundred campsites (don't miss the blufftop sites for elevated views of the lake), swimming area, and the lake packed with various fish. Bring your fishin' pole! And the action doesn't stop in

A gnarly oak flanks the trail DENICE BREAUX

winter. The trails are paradise found for cross-country skiing, snowshoeing, snowmo-biling, and good old-fashioned snowman-making.

Hiking trails here are boulevard-like corridors squiggling throughout the park. Elevation changes run the gamut from pan flat to short, punchy steeps, but overall, the trails are enjoyably exhilarating. This hike follows the Oak Grove loop, with a short connector on the Windy Ridge Trail. The path is flanked by dense hardwood forest of maple, ash, birch, elm, scattered pine, and a handful I couldn't identify. On the subject of trees, the big news at Yellowstone Wildlife Area adjacent to the park is clusters of rare oak savanna, a vestige of the past we are truly blessed to see.

Let's get started! Follow the trail from the road, with a bit of uphill to warm your legs, and take a hard right at the first junction, noodling back southeast on a skinny "tail" of the loop with intermittent views of the lake through the trees. Also serving as cross-country ski trails, most of the park paths are of grassy tread, with occasional sections of dirt doubletrack. Enjoy lots of bright sky through the largely open canopy, with rest stop benches in all the right places, as the trail gradually climbs toward Windy Ridge, passing one connector trail on the right. From the ridge, it's a long downhill cruise with lake views welcoming you back to the trailhead.

Quiet and peaceful every step of the way DENICE BREAUX

Why Go?

No trip to this southern Wisconsin park is complete without a bonus adventure to the adjacent 4,000-acre Yellowstone Wildlife Area. Made of rolling hills of upland grasses, crop fields, and copses of woods, the property is also home to remnant oak savannas, a treasure from the state's rich natural history. Oak savannas, also known as oak barrens, consist of groundcover of grasses and forbs surrounding scattered, open-growth oaks. State officials are actively managing these spaces, once a dominant ecosystem in Wisconsin and other regions of the upper Midwest. In fact, oak savannas once defined roughly 30 percent, nearly seven million acres, of southern Wisconsin's flora. Today, only about 0.01 percent remains.

Miles and Directions

0.0   From the trailhead parking area, follow the road to the Oak Grove Trail and hike northeast away from the lake.

0.4   Turn right at this junction.

1.3   Pass a connector trail on the right.

1.6   Junction with Windy Ridge Trail; turn left and continue hiking south at the Oak Grove Trail split.

2.4   Arrive back at the trailhead.

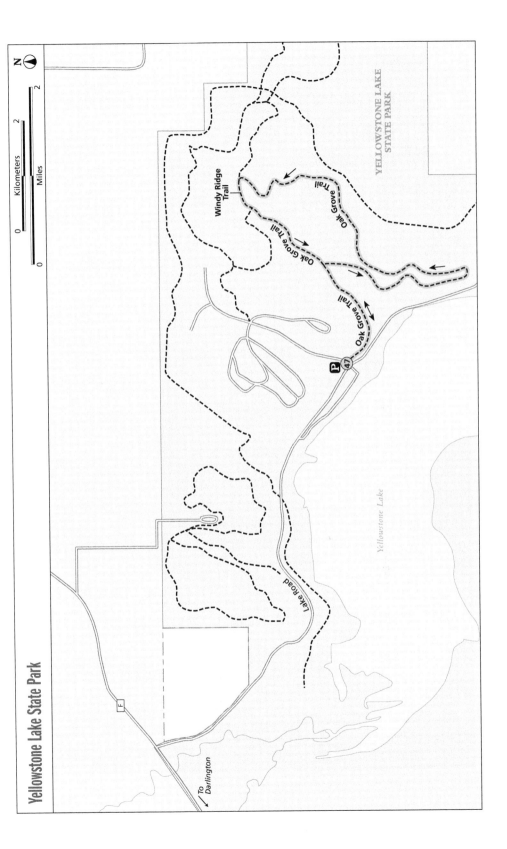

Yellowstone Lake State Park

Windy Ridge Trail

Oak Grove Trail

Oak Grove Trail

Oak Grove Trail

YELLOWSTONE LAKE
STATE PARK

Yellowstone Lake

Lake Road

To
Darlington

N

Kilometers
0   2

Miles
0   2

Distant lake views treat hikers near the end of the hike DENICE BREAUX

Bonus Hikes

If only I had enough days in the year (and pages in this book) to hike all of Wisconsin's best hiking trails and share them with you. Alas, I had to pick and choose among the very best, but these standouts should also make your list:

Kettle Moraine State Forest—Northern Unit

A gem in our state forest system, Kettle Moraine boasts more than 130 miles of multi-use trails, including the Butler Lake Loop winding through a state natural area, shared billing with the Ice Age Trail, and Parnell Tower, 60 feet up and the forest's high point. Trails wander around and over eskers and kettles and moraines—big fun for day hiking and backpacking.

Van Vliet Hemlocks

Go north to Presque Isle to hike among a rare remnant hemlock forest, with old-growth giants, loons on the adjacent lake, songbirds aplenty, and all kinds of wetland and vernal pools.

Pattison State Park

Score choice views of ruggedly elegant Big Manitou Falls and hike bridges and boardwalks on this scenic tour in one of Wisconsin's most popular state parks. At 165 feet, Big Manitou is Wisconsin's highest falls, the fourth tallest east of the Rockies, and at equal height of Niagara Falls. We wouldn't have Big Manitou Falls without this park and if that's not enough, Pattison is also home to more than 200 bird species, fifty-five animal varieties (such as the gray wolf and Blanding's turtle), and rare plants (including the Laurentian Bladder Fern and Northern Yellow Lady's Slipper).

Glacier Trail—Chequamegon National Forest

Shuh-WAH-muh-guhn. Up in these parts, that name is synonymous with more than 1.5 million acres of sublime North Country forest and a lifetime of unforgettable hiking trails. I've hiked and camped all around the country and, home state bias aside, the Chequamegon shares top billing with the very best. There are nowhere near enough superlatives to do this place justice. Indeed, it's nothing short of heaven on earth for hikers and backpackers, with more than 1,000 miles of trails strewn all over Wisconsin's far northern tier like an Etch A Sketch drawing gone wild.

Star Lake

One of the best hikes in the state. A bold statement backed up by ridiculously beautiful scenery, heavenly trails, and conservation-based history. I relished every single step of this hike and more than one time had to pry myself away from one idyllic place only to be captivated by another. For all-around "unforgettableness," this short little hike in northern Wisconsin is tops on the list.

Fallison Lake

A Wisconsin hiking book is not complete without the outrageously beautiful Fallison Lake Trail. With four loop options, old-growth splendor, and a Northwoods-perfect lake, this author favorite is a don't-miss destination for unforgettable trail miles. Go here for an elegantly beautiful forest of white pine, maple, birch, balsam, and aspen; a hemlock glade; bogs and boardwalks, all surrounding a clear northern lake. Even better, this is one of those hidden gems in an already opulent gallery.

Among the bog and hemlock glade environments on this hike, you're in for a treat if the red-eyed vireo is in a singing mood. When not eating insects, larvae, or berries, the vireo sings and really gets into it. This is a great time to just sit still and listen.

Horicon Marsh

Horicon Marsh is a big deal. It's one of the country's largest freshwater marshes, a Wetland of International Importance, and a State and Global Important Bird Area. Lofty credentials indeed, and this is the place to get your wildlife fix. This is real life-list stuff and should be way up on your hiking must-do list. Well over 33,000 acres, the marsh (the largest freshwater cattail marsh in the US) is critical habitat for more than 300 species of birds, far too many to even begin to list here, as well as other critters such as red foxes, frogs, toads, bats, muskrat, fish, and turtles.

Interstate State Park

Hands down some of the most scenic views in the state can be found in this park. A proud claim perhaps, but one look at the Dalles of the St. Croix and you'll agree this is a very special place. The first time I saw the Dalles, I was sure I'd been transported to Middle Earth. I stood there transfixed. It could've been 5 minutes or 30 and it didn't matter; I was wholly absorbed by the wild, unadulterated, fantasy world magic of the place, and if I wasn't at my desk writing this book, I'd be back out there.

I have nowhere near enough superlatives (they would fall far short anyway) to describe what the Dalles is all about. It will reach a part of you that perhaps hasn't been reached before and will leave you inspired by far more than its physical beauty. But in the meantime, give thanks with verve that you are able to be part of something like this if only for a brief moment.

Perrot State Park

This lumpy park in Wisconsin's southwest is home to the confluence of the Trempealeau and Mississippi Rivers and sublime views of the valley from Perrot Ridge or Brady's Bluff.

Think back 500 million years or so when an enormous inland sea covered today's Wisconsin. All that water drained as the land rose, and later another sea moved in. The advance and retreat of these inland seas piled up lots of mud and debris, creating the dramatic sandstone bluffs of today's Perrot State Park. Many of these steep, lumpy

Stop and stay a while DENICE BREAUX

bluffs rise to more than 500 feet above verdant wetlands, open fields, and deep valleys; providing homes to hundreds of flora and fauna species.

Habitat loss and fragmentation are among the leading adversaries of wildlife's drive to survive, and Perrot State Park is akin to an island of walnut, hickory, and old-growth oak that support birds such as the pileated woodpecker, scarlet tanager, and many of their kin. A 2018 land donation to the Mississippi Valley Conservancy added 18 acres of ecologically significant land abutting the park that augments critical habitat of migratory songbirds along the Mississippi River.

Gibraltar Rock State Natural Area

This hike to the top of Gibraltar Rock rewards with exhilarating, panoramic views of the Wisconsin River Valley, Lake Wisconsin, and the far-off Baraboo Hills. This is our humble midwestern counterpart to the fabled Rock of Gibraltar on the southern tip of Europe's Iberian Peninsula. On your hike, watch for ever-present raptors. With only the slightest quiver of a wing, the great birds float on thermals created by Gibraltar Rock's warm cliff face, high above the dark green canopy of red cedar. Below the trees is a veritable circus of groundcover grasses, including big and little bluestem, prairie drop-seed, bird's foot violet, prairie smoke, milkweed, goldenrod, and much more.

Meet the Author

Steve Johnson is a self-propelled recreation junkie and fan of all things outdoors. He is a contributor to *Backpacker* and regional magazines across the country and creates destination guides for *National Geographic*. Some of Steve's other work includes *Hiking Waterfalls in Minnesota, Best Lake Hikes Wisconsin,* and *Best Easy Bike Rides Minneapolis and Saint Paul*. Steve lives and writes at a cabin in northern Wisconsin.

Meet the Photographers

A native Californian, writer-photographer Denice Breaux is a recent Twin Cities transplant, and what better way to get acquainted with the Midwest than plunging into Wisconsin's glorious outdoors? Along the way she has become intimately familiar with chilblains, chiggers, and voracious mosquitoes, a few things not experienced on the West Coast. See more images from this book at Denice's website, denicebreauxphoto.com. Her portfolio of stock images can be viewed at istockphoto.com/portfolio/DeniceBreaux.

Kent Merhar is a semiprofessional photographer with a career in health-care administration. His focus is landscape photography. When he's not outdoors hiking or enjoying a long weekend at his cabin, he's at his Minneapolis home with his partner and dog. See more of his work at facebook.com/unknownlimitsphotography.

THE TEN ESSENTIALS OF HIKING

American
Hiking
Society

American Hiking Society recommends you pack the "Ten Essentials" every time you head out for a hike. Whether you plan to be gone for a couple of hours or several months, make sure to pack these items. Become familiar with these items and know how to use them. Learn more at **AmericanHiking.org/hiking-resources**

 1. **Appropriate Footwear**

 6. **Safety Items** (light, fire, and a whistle)

 2. **Navigation**

 7. **First Aid Kit**

 3. **Water** (and a way to purify it)

 8. **Knife or Multi-Tool**

 4. **Food**

 9. **Sun Protection**

 5. **Rain Gear & Dry-Fast Layers**

 10. **Shelter**

PROTECT THE PLACES YOU LOVE TO HIKE

Become a member today and take $5 off an annual membership using the code **Falcon5**.

AmericanHiking.org/join

American Hiking Society is the only national nonprofit organization dedicated to empowering all to enjoy, share, and preserve the hiking experience.